Strategies for Readers

A Reading/Communication Text for Students of ESL

Book 1

Christine Pearson Casanave

Stanford University

Prentice-Hall, Englewood Cliffs, New Jersey 07632

Library of Congress Cataloging-in-Publication Data

Casanave, Christine Pearson, 1944–
   Strategies for readers.

   Includes index.
   1. College readers. 2. English language—Textbooks
for foreign speakers. I. Title.
PE1122.C353 1986   428.6'4   85-19444
ISBN 0-13-850728-7

Cover Design: Joe Curcio
Manufacturing Buyer: Harry P. Baisley
Illustrator: Christine Pearson Casanave

© 1986 by Prentice-Hall
A Division of Simon & Schuster, Inc.
Englewood Cliffs, New Jersey 07632

Printed in the United States of America

10 9 8 7 6 5 4 3 2 1

ISBN 0-13-850728-7   01

Prentice-Hall International (UK) Limited, *London*
Prentice-Hall of Australia Pty. Limited, *Sydney*
Prentice-Hall Canada Inc., *Toronto*
Prentice-Hall Hispanoamericana, S.A., *Mexico*
Prentice-Hall of India Private Limited, *New Delhi*
Prentice-Hall of Japan, Inc., *Tokyo*
Prentice-Hall of Southeast Asia Pte. Ltd., *Singapore*
Editora Prentice-Hall do Brasil, Ltda., *Rio de Janeiro*
Whitehall Books Limited, *Wellington, New Zealand*

Table of Contents

Preface

Strategies for Readers, Book 1 (henceforth *Strategies 1*) is a low-intermediate reading and communication text for young adult and adult students of English as a second language (ESL). It is designed for use in college and university ESL programs that prepare students to use English as the medium for study and work. The topics are concrete and familiar. Their treatment, however, is academic and conceptual. *Strategies for Readers, Book 2 (Strategies 2),* the second volume in the set, follows the same approach and format, but the topics increase in abstractness, length, and difficulty. There are ten to sixteen exercises per chapter. Each volume is complete under one cover: The texts include student material as well as instructions to teachers in the form of a special teacher's introduction and within-text notes. (An Answer Key is published separately.) The abundance and variety of activities give teachers and administrators the flexibility to adapt each text to an eight- or ten-week term, and to cover all or part of both volumes in a ten- or fifteen-week term.

Strategies 1 and *2* can be used most effectively in the reading class, though the oral and reading activities could be divided between two teachers. However, the communicative prereading activities are intended to provide students with an immediate foundation for the reading activities in each chapter, and to help them see the commonality in thinking and decision-making processes in oral communication and in reading. Where possible, the same teacher should use the text with the same group of students.

Students of ESL know a great deal. They have a lifetime of experience behind them. One of the purposes of *Strategies 1* and *2* is to activate this knowledge and allow it to contribute both to language acquisition and to reading comprehension. *Strategies 1* gives students some tools with which to think, talk, and read about familiar objects. *Strategies 2* does the same for familiar places and phenomena.

Both volumes ask students to think, compare, solve problems, and communicate their own ideas. Students will work closely with other students and with their teacher. They will practice many different reading strategies in a variety of formats. They will learn to bring their own knowledge to the reading task. Students and teachers will be reminded that sometimes answers are not clearly right or wrong, even in a textbook, and that in reading, as in life, issues can be interpreted in more than one way. Many factors, including cultural ones, help determine which solutions seem more logical than others.

Thus, it is important for those who use *Strategies 1* and *2* to be flexible in their interpretation of what is "correct" and "incorrect."

Teachers: As you use this book, pick and choose exercises and activities that fit the needs and the interests of your students. The vocabulary in each chapter is recycled, making an orderly progression through the material beneficial to students. But the exercises are there for you to use as you see fit. Supplement with outside readings on topics of special interest as your time allows. Above all, remember that interest is generated by active involvement in and successful completion of activities: Nothing motivates like success.

Acknowledgments

Many people helped in the development and production of *Strategies for Readers*. I thank Debbie Wren for classroom testing the first draft chapters, Mimi Corneli and Diane Williams for their drafts of several of the reading articles and for their valuable suggestions on many other chapters, and Jean Zukowski/Faust for sharing with me her love of and commitment to the field of second language reading and materials development. I appreciate the support provided me by the Monterey Institute of International Studies as I developed these materials and the cooperation of the Institute's ESL students during classroom testing. Special thanks to Eleanor Pearson for her careful typing and proofing of many chapters, and to Robin Baliszewski and Barbara Bernstein at Prentice-Hall and to Genie Dailey at Aspen Hollow Artservice for their time and talent during all phases of production. Finally, to those close to me who supported me even at my crabbiest, I express my love and gratitude.

CRPC
Monterey, California
July 1985

Dedicated to J.

Information for Teachers

This section and the notes to teachers within the text constitute the "teacher's manual" for **Strategies 1** and **2**. This arrangement has not been tried before. If teachers have comments or suggestions, they may write to Editor, ESL, Prentice-Hall, Englewood Cliffs, NJ 07632.

SUMMARY OF KEY POINTS

- Utilize students' knowledge and experience.
- Use oral activities as a foundation for reading activities.
- *Plan ahead* for prereading activities.
- Work through the main reading article *quickly*, and make the final two readings in each chapter your *goal*.
- Pick and choose exercises as needed.
- Instruct students in the purposes and procedures of small group work.
- Involve students actively with the exercises, with each other, and with you.

PLANNING

With planning and flexibility, each volume of **Strategies for Readers** can be adapted to programs of eight or ten weeks. The two volumes can usually be covered in a fifteen-week semester. Some teachers may wish to do four or five chapters from each volume in a quarter. A typical plan would have the reading teacher use **Strategies** in a five-hour block per week. The prereading activities would take one or two hours, and the readings and exercises would fill the remaining hours. If it is absolutely necessary to divide activities between two teachers, coordinate activities closely, since the oral activities are the foundation for the reading activities.

Some prereading activities may require advance planning. Read ahead to see what is needed in terms of realia, pictures, and so on. All planning in **Strategies** is easy, but it may require a little extra time. Scan the chapter before you teach so that you can quickly choose or eliminate exercises to suit your schedule and your group.

ORGANIZATION OF *STRATEGIES 1* AND *2*

Strategies for Readers is a two volume set. *Strategies 1* has two main parts—*Introductions* and *Things*—and a total of six chapters. *Strategies 2* has two parts—*Places* and *Phenomena*—and eight chapters. The progression of parts and chapters is from concrete, here-and-now topics in volume 1 to topics in volume 2 that are more abstract. Each chapter is divided into four parts: prereading activities, main reading, exercises plus a final communicative activity, and extra readings.

Vocabulary is recycled within chapters, from one chapter to the next, and from *Strategies 1* to *Strategies 2*. Students learn new words by practicing them in a variety of contexts. There are no vocabulary lists beyond the list of Key Words with each main reading. The style of writing is simple and natural. Readings have not been artificially adapted or controlled; normal redundancies and connections have been left in. It is hoped that what students lack in knowledge of syntax they will in part make up for by their existing knowledge of the topic and their developing knowledge of vocabulary. Increasing proficiency in syntax comes in through the back door, so to speak.

Let us look now at some specific features of this text.

Prereading

The extensive PREREADING section in each chapter is a unique feature of *Strategies for Readers,* and teachers are urged to spend some time with it. The rationale behind this recommendation is grounded in psycholinguistic and schema-theoretic conceptualizations of reading, which emphasize the role of the reader's knowledge and experience in the reading task. In this text, the prereading activities help students activate this knowledge.

The PREREADING section is divided into two parts. One is a *communicative activity* that is designed to activate students' background knowledge in a certain area and to provide vocabulary. *Strategies 2* offers a choice of two communicative activities in each chapter, thus affording teachers the flexibility to fit the activity to individual groups. The second part involves *interaction with the reading article* and asks students to survey, scan, underline, skim, predict, and question.

No text, including this one, teaches itself, and most of the communicative prereading activities require some preparation. **Read ahead** to see if the addition of realia or pictures is crucial. It is the real contact with objects and ideas that makes the lessons in both volumes of *Strategies* meaningful and interesting for students, and that facilitates vocabulary acquisition in particular and language acquisition in general. In accordance with recent theories of language and reading acquisition, the communicative prereading activities require real language use, active involvement of students, and activation of student knowledge and experience. These activities can be absorbing; if you are pressed for time, it may be wise to give students a time limit.

The Key Words list in the second part of the PREREADING is written in such a way as to provide a skeletal overview of the reading article. Some words and phrases are indented to indicate their relation to previous items. Numbers to the left correspond to paragraph numbers in the article. This list can be used in any way the teacher and students wish—as the basis for the Underline task, as a quick overview of the article, as a mnemonic for students in retelling tasks, as a study device, and so on. Appendix 2 provides an alphabetical list of all Key Words and footnote vocabulary in the book, coded by chapter number. Teachers and students may use the Appendix in any way they wish—for example, as a reference for locating a particular word, for checking spellings, and for monitoring development of vocabulary for recognition. For this latter purpose, students could periodically go through the list and check off words that they recognize. Please remind students that they should not try to memorize this list!

The two kinds of Underline exercises may require a little time to learn to use smoothly. In *Strategies 1,* students underline what they hear. In *Strategies 2,* students underline answers to questions asked by the teacher. You may decide to use the Underline exercise, adapt it, or eliminate it, according to the needs of each class. Underlining is a very personal matter. Some readers do it more than others. Some readers prefer to take notes, or they may have a different system altogether. However, students need to understand the rationale behind underlining, which is a means of highlighting important information for quick future reference. At least some practice at this task is highly recommended.

In the PREREADING section, the strategies of surveying, scanning, skimming, and predicting are used to help students build expectations about what they are going to read. The first three terms can be confusing because people use them interchangeably. In *Strategies for Readers, surveying* refers to a first glance at an article or chapter to see what is there. Students will need to look at titles, headings, illustrations—the obvious features. *Strategies* distinguishes between *scanning*—moving the eyes quickly over reading matter in search of a specific bit of information—and *skimming,* which might be considered an "in-depth" survey—a quick look at a whole article to get a general idea of what it is about.

Not all of these activities will be equally important for individual students or for all reading articles. By being familiar with the reading article and with their students, teachers will be able to decide which of these activities to emphasize, adapt, or eliminate. Teachers should not feel obligated to cover all sections with equal attention.

The Listen exercise allows students to read silently, yet still make important sound-symbol correspondences as the teacher reads. Students will also get a sense of the syntax of each sentence by hearing intonation and stress. Some teachers may feel they can push students to read faster silently by increasing the rate at which students hear the oral reading. The Listen activity, too, may be more important for some students than for others.

Finally, the instructions in the SILENT READING section ask students to read for a purpose—for example, to answer questions that are given or that students themselves have composed, or to compare what they read with their own experience.

Main Readings

All of the main readings in *Strategies 1* and *2* are on topics with which students should have some familiarity even before they do the prereading activities. In other words, very little new information is presented. After doing the prereading activities, students will be familiar not only with the topic, but with the vocabulary and structural features of the article. Therefore, **work through this main reading quickly** to give students a successful experience with fast, fluent reading and to prevent boredom.

Many of the main readings utilize the following features of academic prose: headings and subheadings, footnote format for vocabulary glosses, tables, and (in *Strategies 2*) diagrams and graphs. Less academic readings include an interview, a journal, and a first-person narrative.

Exercises

Approximately twenty basic exercise types, with variations, are used in the two volumes of *Strategies for Readers*. All exercises give students practice with different strategies that good readers use, such as categorizing, inferring, guessing, understanding cohesive devices, predicting, reading in logical word groups, and distinguishing facts from opinions. These exercises also reinforce previously introduced vocabulary and topics, help students recognize characteristically Western ways of thinking, stimulate communicative language use, and acquaint students with common academic tasks such as paraphrasing, summarizing, organizing, and so forth. In short, the exercises give students the opportunity to think, to talk, to weigh and compare ideas with other students and with the teacher, and to read.

Following is an overview of some specific activities and exercises.

Directions. All activities and exercises in both volumes of *Strategies* begin with directions. *The directions should be considered reading matter.* The ability to read and understand directions is perhaps the most basic of the reading abilities our students must acquire. Review all directions carefully with students. If you do small group activities, be sure to review directions *before* the class is divided up: You will save yourself many repetitions.

Comprehension Check and Selective Reading. Every chapter has two or three different Comprehension Checks and Selective Readings. Faster, more advanced students will be able to do all of them. Select one or two of each for slower students. Comprehension Checks such as true-false and multiple choice exercises give students practice with these traditional test-taking formats. More holistic checks are those that involve retelling, summarizing, and discussing.

With the exception of those in the first two chapters of *Strategies 1,* the Selective Readings focus on meaning rather than on visual discrimination. These exercises require students to think in terms of categories, to move their eyes from left to right (teachers need to remind students of this), and to push themselves to work quickly.

Other Exercises. Teachers may pick and choose from the other exercises in each chapter as needed and as time permits. They are not ordered in any strict way, and teachers should feel free to establish their own sequencing. Some exercises are coded to indicate that they are being introduced for the first time (see List of Symbols at the end of Information for Teachers). These unfamiliar exercises may require more introductory explanation. (The author recommends "explanation" by exemplification at this level.)

The exercises can be classified in three main groups: those that are closely tied to the text, those that are tied to the text but require more risk or interpretation, and those that depend on students' own knowledge and interests.

1. Exercises That Are Tied to the Text. The following exercise types fall into this category: Logical Word Groups, Levels of Generalization, Reference, Connectors, Scan, Order, Analogies, Paraphrase, Reading Charts and Graphs, and Summarize. Most of these exercises ask students to *read* and *recognize,* not to write. Even the paraphrase exercise is one of recognition: Students must determine whether two sentences have similar or different meanings. Logical Word Groups helps students understand the importance of perceiving grammatically related groups of words while reading. The Order exercises ask students to reorder randomly organized words and sentences in various kinds of sequence—alphabetical, numerical, chronological, and so on. At the sentence level, such exercises can be turned into a communicative activity if they are done as "strip stories." *

The Reference exercises are perhaps the most important in this group. (In this book, the term *reference* includes any cohesive device that allows us to say that X refers to Y.) This text does not begin to cover all the kinds of cohesive ties that students need to know, and does not even introduce the concept of coherence. But the exercises do cover basic pronoun reference and lexical substitution.

2. Exercises That Require Risk and Interpretation. These exercises—Guess, Predict, Making Inferences, and Fact or Opinion—involve a certain amount of ambiguity and thus obligate students to take some risks in order to find a satisfactory answer. Students and teachers both must be prepared for some discomfort, some disagreement, and a lot of discussion, because answers are not always clearly black or white. Even if more than one answer is theoretically possible, teachers must help students understand which are more *logically* possible, given a Western context. It is best to avoid labels such as "right" or "wrong" for responses to certain of these exercises, and to call them instead more or less logical.

3. Exercises That Depend on Students' Knowledge and Interests. The following exercises have no best answer at all, but depend solely on what students bring to them: Word Association, Vocabulary Study, Agree/Disagree, Discuss, Reflection (at the end of the timed Extra Reading), and all opinion and personal knowledge items. Such exercises are powerful equalizers in multilevel classes, and they can pull the quietest of students into discussions. In the Word Association and Vocabulary Study exercises, students are at liberty to choose their own words. In the others, their own opinions and ideas are the only "right" answers.

Activity. An activity follows the exercises. Like the prereading activity, it is communicative and usually requires students to utilize their own knowledge, interests, and

---

* "Strip stories" require some preparation, but the time is well spent. Write or type each sentence on a separate index card. Hand one or more cards out to each student. Ask students to memorize their sentence(s) and then turn in their cards (or keep them and read from them). Students must then organize themselves into the proper sequence, without help from the teacher, and conclude with a full recitation of the paragraph. If teachers let students figure out how to carry out this task, a great deal of communication will take place.

opinions. This final activity can be a valuable language acquisition tool as well as an enjoyable conclusion to the exercise section.

Extra Readings. The two final readings at the end of each chapter are a goal toward which all students should aim. Students have a chance to put together what they have practiced in previous chapters, without the pressure of comprehension checks, and to think and talk about what they read in more holistic terms. The first of the extra readings is on a topic that is somewhat related to the main reading and thus should be familiar to students. It can be timed, and students can figure out their reading rate (see instructions in Appendix 1). Teachers may wish to have students look at the Reflection questions (at the end of the reading) *before* they read, as a prereading activation of knowledge. (**Note:** Because the Extra Readings are not of comparable difficulty or style, a "progress chart" that records increases [or decreases] in reading rate over time may not reflect real progress.)

The second Extra Reading uses familiar vocabulary in an unfamiliar context and format. Students can profit by working together to answer the follow-up questions, which rely heavily on their prior knowledge and their ability to make inferences.

OTHER ISSUES

Small Group Work

Strategies 1 and *2* encourage the use of small group work whenever possible on the assumption that people (not just students!) can think better, learn more, and arrive at better solutions when they work together. Very few activities in life require us to work as solitary individuals. All of us regularly consult, confer, and discuss with those around us.

Our students will need to *learn* how to work in small groups, however, since most of them are probably not accustomed to this style of work in a classroom setting. Most students come to the classroom with strong expectations about student and teacher roles; small group work and student-centered activities may clash with their norms about classroom behavior.

Teachers can alleviate student discomfort by making sure that students are thoroughly acquainted with each other, including knowing and using names, from the first week of class. Many get-acquainted games can be devised for this purpose. Teachers should also instruct students carefully in the purposes and procedures of small group work. Finally, teachers can strengthen small group work by continually making students aware that each one of them brings to the group valuable knowledge and experience.

A word of caution: Teachers should be aware that some cultures and some individuals do not consider the sharing of personal information appropriate. Treat such situations sensitively and flexibly. Teachers who do not wish to use small group work can easily conduct all exercises in a whole-class task structure. In fact, such a task structure is sometimes more appropriate for the culturally homogeneous class.

Reading Aloud

In the PREREADING section of each chapter in both volumes of ***Strategies for Readers,*** the teacher is asked to read aloud to the students from the reading article while students follow in their books. In this way, students practice both silent reading and sound–symbol correspondence at the same time. (Do not assume that, just because students have used some of the same words fluently in the prereading activity, they will recognize them in their printed form!) They will also hear, through the teacher's phrasing, how sentences become meaningful when they are perceived in logical (i.e., grammatical) word groups.

Many students enjoy reading aloud, too. However, they may mistakenly believe that oral reading is necessary to learn to read well, and that it reflects how we read silently (it probably doesn't). The goal of the two volumes of ***Strategies*** is to help students learn to read silently and efficiently. Oral reading can be used for other purposes, of course—pronunciation and phrasing practice, for example, or for reading matter that is more oral in nature, such as first-person accounts and interviews. Oral reading of *directions* is recommended, at least in the early chapters of each volume.

Tests

No tests are provided with this text, which is primarily a practice book. If teachers need them, tests can be written to fit each group of students. Items can be modeled on or taken from exercises in the book, the Extra Readings can be used, or cloze tests can be written from the reading articles.

Answer Key

An Answer Key is provided (under separate cover) for some of the exercises. Because the focus of ***Strategies for Readers*** is on the *processes* of finding answers and comprehending reading matter, and not on right or wrong answers themselves, teachers should view the Answer Key as a guide, not a goal. Answers to tasks that have ambiguous or personal solutions are not listed in the Answer Key, nor are choices in most Selective Reading exercises and strip stories.

Teacher's Manual

You have just read half of the teacher's manual. A convenient feature of ***Strategies 1*** and ***2*** is that there is no separate teacher's manual: All information for teachers is included under one cover. In addition to the general information you have just read, detailed teaching suggestions can be found within the body of the text itself—in small print set off by rules.

List of Exercises
by Chapter and Kind

⊛ = new

Part 1: Introductions

Chapter 1: Names

- ⊛ A. Comprehension Check: True or False
- ⊛ B. Comprehension Check: Multiple Choice
- ⊛ C. Comprehension Check: Discuss
- ⊛ D. Selective Reading: Underline Same Words
- ⊛ E. Selective Reading: Cross Out Different Words
- ⊛ F. Selective Reading: Circle Numbers
- ⊛ G. Selective Reading: Underline Examples
- ⊛ H. Reading Charts and Tables
- ⊛ I. Paraphrase
- ⊛ J. Reference: *it, they, them*
- ⊛ K. Activity: Filling in a Chart

Chapter 2: Textbooks

-   A. Comprehension Check: True or False
-   B. Comprehension Check: Multiple Choice
- ⊛ C. Comprehension Check: Answer
-   D. Selective Reading: Underline Same Words
-   E. Selective Reading: Cross Out Different Phrases
-   F. Selective Reading: Cross Out Unrelated Word
- ⊛ G. Logical Word Groups
- ⊛ H. Order: Alphabetical
-   I. Reference· *it, they, them*
-   J. Paraphrase
- ⊛ K. Outlining
- ⊛ L. Activity: Looking at Books and Magazines from Your Country

Part 2: Things

List of Abbreviations and Symbols

n	noun
v	verb
adj	adjective
adv	adverb
prep	preposition
expr	expression; idiom
sing	singular
pl	plural
C	countable noun
U	uncountable noun

*	There is a note of explanation on this page.
=	*means; is*
. . .	Some words from a sentence have been left out.
⊛	new exercise
Ⓟ	PLAN AHEAD!

Part 1

Introductions

Part 1 is very short. It has only two (2) chapters. The purpose of Part 1 is to introduce you to each other and to introduce you to this book. Both Chapter 1, "Names," and Chapter 2, "Textbooks," help you learn how to use this book. You do not need to understand every word in the chapters. It is more important in these chapters to learn how to do the exercises. Your teacher will help you.

Now, think about these questions:

Who are my classmates (the other students in the class)?

What kinds of exercises are in this book?

Teacher: This section contains the models and explanations for several of the basic exercise types used in this book. Although the chapters may seem difficult for your students, especially Chapter 2, remember that students do not need to read and comprehend all the directions and explanations at this point. Likewise, they should not be asked to remember all the terminology. However, they do need to know how to **do** the activities, which are designed to teach reading strategies. With your guidance, they will complete these activities successfully.

Chapter 1
Names

PREREADING

Ⓟ **Activity:** Getting to Know Each Other

Materials: Index cards (two or three per student), felt pens, one or two boxes to put index cards in.

- **Directions:**

Teacher: Write your full name on an index card. Explain your name to the class. Then write what you wish your class to call you on another card. Show the class. ("Please call me _____.")
    Then guide students through the following steps.

1. What is your family (last) name? What is your given (first) name? Write your first name and your last name on an index card. Write in large, clear letters.

2. What name do you want to be called in this class? Write this name on another index card. This is your class name card.

3. Introduce yourselves. "My name is _____ _____. Please call me _____."

4. Choose one or more of the next "games."

Teacher: These get-acquainted games can be done over several days. Add others as needed.

---

   a. Exchange cards with your classmates (= the people you are studying with). Explain your names to each other: "This is my first name. This is my last name. You can call me _____."

   b. Put all of the index cards (full name cards and class name cards) into a box. Mix them up. Then have one student at a time pick a card and read the name out loud. That student has to find the person and return the card to him or her.

   c. Make two teams. Put all the class name cards from the first team (Team A) into a box. Put all the class name cards from the second team (Team B) into another box. Exchange boxes: Team A has Team B's names; Team B has Team A's names. Take turns drawing names. Match each name with the correct person on the opposite team. Give one point for each correct match. The team with the most points wins.

   d. Interview each other. Find out full name and class name. Find out home country and native language. Find out interests. Introduce each other in class: "This is _____. Please call him (her) _____. He (She) is from _____. He (She) speaks _____. He (She) is interested in _____."

Teacher: Be sure to encourage everyone from this point on to use names in class!

Survey

Teacher: If necessary, demonstrate to students where to find answers. You may wish to explain the terms *survey, scan, skim,* and *underline* now (see Information for Teachers) or postpone explanation until students are more familiar with the text.

■ **Directions:** Your teacher will ask you some questions. Write your answers on a piece of paper or answer orally.

1. Look at the picture (a cartoon) at the beginning of this chapter. Who are the people? (Guess.) What are they doing?

2. Turn to the beginning of the reading article "NAMES." Find the word NAMES at the top of the page. This word is the **title** of the article.

3. Look on the left side of the page. Are there any numbers? These numbers are **paragraph numbers.** How many paragraph numbers are there?

4. Look above paragraph number 1. Find the word INTRODUCTION. It is in large capital letters. The word INTRODUCTION is a **heading.** It introduces a new section. Look above the other numbers. Are there more headings?

5. Copy all the headings on your paper (or give them orally).

Scan

■ **Directions:** Look at the article. Follow these directions from your teacher. Find the answers as quickly as possible.

1. Find the heading NICKNAMES. In this section, find the lists of names for men and women. What is the nickname for James (man)? What is the nickname for Patricia (woman)?

2. Find the heading LAST NAMES. In this section, find the two lists of last names. What is one example of an English name? What is one example of a non-English name? What is the origin of the non-English name that you picked?

Key Words

■ **Directions:** Read the list of key words and phrases. They are important words and phrases in the reading article "NAMES." The numbers are paragraph numbers. Can you get an idea about the article by reading this list?

1 English speakers
   three names
   first name . . . middle name . . . last
      name
2 Americans like first names.
3 nickname
   informal form of a first name
4 some first names . . .
   do not have a nickname form

5 middle names are common
6 last name . . . family name
   many American family names . . .
   not of English origin
7 title . . . a label
8 titles . . . used only with last names

Listen

■ **Directions:** Listen while your teacher reads all or part of the article out loud. Follow silently in your book.

Underline

■ **Directions:** Your teacher will read the Key Words to you from paragraphs 1, 2, and 3 of the article. When you hear the words, find them in the paragraph and underline them. Do the following example first. The first Key Words are underlined for you.

Teacher: (See Chapter 2 for a more complete demonstration and explanation.) Demonstrate underlining with the following example from paragraph 1 of the reading article. Give the paragraph number, then read each set of Key Words. Pause long enough after each set for students to find the phrase and underline it. **Note.** Ⓟ Underline the Key Words in your own copy of the text and work from the article itself for all underlining exercises like this one.

Teacher (Key Words)

1   English speakers
    three names
    first name . . . middle name . . . last name

Student (Underline)

1   Everyone has a name. In fact, most people have more than one name. For example, most Americans, and many other native <u>English speakers</u>, have three names: a first name (given name), a middle name, and a last name (surname or family name).

Skim

■ **Directions:** Go to the beginning of the article "NAMES." Read the following parts of the article:
  a. the introduction (paragraph 1)
  b. all of the headings
  c. your underlined words
  d. the conclusion (paragraph 9)

Predict

■ **Directions:** Choose the best answer to complete the statement.

The main idea (basic, most important information) in the article "NAMES" is probably going to be about _____.

  a. the origins of names
  b. the first, middle, and last names of English speakers such as Americans
  c. titles, such as Dr., Mrs., and Mr.

SILENT READING

■ **Directions:** Before you read, think about these questions:

How do you use names in your country? Do you use first names? Middle names? Last names? Titles? Do you use different names in different situations? Is the system of names in your country different from the system that is described in the article? Be prepared to talk about these questions after you read.

Now read the entire article silently and carefully. Read as quickly as you can.

NAMES

INTRODUCTION

1   Everyone has a name. In fact, most people have more than one name. For example, most Americans, and many other native English speakers, have three names: a first name (given name), a middle name, and a last name (surname or family name).

EXAMPLE: Diane   Marie   Williams
          first name   middle name last name

FIRST NAMES

2   *Bill, Bob, Tom,* and *John* are common first names in English for men. *Nancy, Mary,* and *Susan* are common first names for women. Americans like first names. Friends, family members, and people who work together use first names with each other. Everybody uses first names with children. Teachers usually use first names with their students. Americans use first names a lot, perhaps more than people from other countries use them.

NICKNAMES

3   A nickname is a familiar or informal form of a first name. For example, *William* is a common first name for a man. *Bill* (also *Billy* or *Will*) is a nickname for *William*. Americans use nicknames more often than complete first names. Table 1 lists some common first names for men and women, and their nicknames (in alphabetical order).

4   Some first names, however, do not ordinarily have a nickname form. *Carol, Ann,* and *Mary* are examples of names for women that do not have common nickname forms. *Paul, Keith,* and *Mark* are three common names for men that do not usually have nicknames.

MIDDLE NAMES

5   Middle names are common in English, but they are not universal. In other words, most native speakers of English have middle names, but not all of them

Table 1. List of First Names and Nicknames

MEN		WOMEN	
Name	Nickname	Name	Nickname
Arthur	Art	Deborah	Debbie
David	Dave	Elizabeth	Liz; Betty
James	Jim	Jennifer	Jenny
Richard	Dick	Kathleen	Kathy
Robert	Bob	Margaret	Marge; Maggie; Meg
Thomas	Tom	Patricia	Pat; Patty
William	Bill	Susan	Sue; Susie

do. Many middle names are similar in kind to first names: *Elizabeth, William,* and *Robert.* Some middle names are the same as the first, middle, or last name of someone in the family—a grandmother, for example. We do not use the nickname forms of middle names. In fact, we do not often use full middle names except on forms (documents, applications). Middle *initials,* however, are common: John *W.* Davis.

LAST NAMES

6   The last name in English is the family name. It is from the father's side of the family. A wife usually takes the family name of her husband, and the children have their father's last name. Last names are interesting because they show something about the origin of a family. Many American family names, for example, are not of English origin.

Table 2. List of Last Names: English and Non-English

English Origin	Non-English Origin - - - - - → Origin	
Baker	Bigley	Irish
Carpenter	Costanza	Italian
Davis	Chong	Chinese
Johnson	Habib	Lebanese
Jones	Nakamoto	Japanese
Smith	Ramirez	Spanish
Taylor	Dumont	French
Wood	Wilke	German

TITLES

7   A title is a label that tells something about a person. We know that *Mr.* Davis is a man. We know that *Mrs.* Williams is a married woman. *Miss* Rogers and *Ms.* Costanza are both women. We know that *Miss* Rogers is single, but we

do not know from the title if *Ms.* Costanza is married or single. *Dr.* Bigley is a doctor, a dentist, or a professor—we do not know exactly from the title. Also, we do not know if Dr. Bigley is a man or a woman.

8   In general, titles are used only with last names: Mr. Harris, Dr. Wood, Miss Dumont. Children use titles and last names with adults who are not relatives. Most students use titles and last names with their teachers. Most people use titles with the names of professors, doctors, lawyers, and other professional people. It is not common to use only titles when we speak with people.

CONCLUSION

9   Let us conclude this short article on names by looking at one name. This person is a married woman who is a college teacher. You will recognize the name from the introduction: *Diane Marie Williams.*

First Name: Diane	Used by her teachers, classmates, friends. *Not* used with titles.
Nickname: Di	Used by her family, close friends.
Middle Name: Marie	Used on documents, application forms.
Middle Initial: M.	Used on many kinds of written forms, in her signature.
Last Name: Williams	Used with her first name, with a title.
Title: Mrs., Ms.	Used with her last name. Used by her students and in formal situations.

EXERCISES _____

(✱)

A. COMPREHENSION CHECK: True or False

■ **Directions:**   Write T after the statements that are true according to the article. Write F after the statements that are false (not true).

1. This article has both an introduction and a conclusion.   _____

2. Most Americans have only two names: a first name and a last name.   _____

3. Americans use first names in many different situations.   _____

4. A nickname is an informal name.   _____

5. American last names originated in many different countries of the world.   _____

6. Americans like to use middle names.   _____

7. Titles like *Mr., Mrs., Miss,* and *Dr.* are not used with first names. _____

8. This article talks about different ways of using names. _____

B. COMPREHENSION CHECK: Multiple Choice

■ Directions: Choose the best answer. Write the letter in the blank. (Number 5 is **not** from the reading article.)

1. Bill is a common _____.

    a. first name   b. middle name   c. last name

2. _____ are very popular in the United States.

    a. Middle names   b. Middle initials   c. Nicknames

3. Americans probably use _____ more often than people from some other countries do.

    a. titles   b. middle names   c. first names

4. In English, last names are from the _____ side of the family.

    a. mother's   b. father's   c. grandmother's

5. We use a _____ with the teacher of this class.

    a. first name   b. nickname   c. title and last name

C. COMPREHENSION CHECK: Discuss

■ Directions: Go back to the questions in SILENT READING (just before the article). Discuss some of them in class. Be sure to compare the system of names in your country with the system that is described in the article.

D. SELECTIVE READING: Underline Same Words

■ Directions: Look at the word on the left. Underline the same word(s) in the line. Move your eyes from left to right (L ⟶ R). Work as quickly as possible.

    EXAMPLE: two: too   to   toe   <u>two</u>   town   <u>two</u>

1. first: flirt   fast   first   fist   thirst   first   birth   frost

2. speaker: speak   speaker   speech   speaking   sneaker   teacher
steak

3. middle: middle   nibble   meddle   middle   wiggle   midlife
mitten

4. common: commonly   comma   come   common   common
come on   coming

5. name: mane   name   wane   man   manner   name   namer
name   fame

6. initial: initial   initiate   imitate   initial   invite   initials
initialize

7. Johnson: Jonson   Johnsen   Jones   Thompson   Johnson
Johnston   Johnson

8. title: titter   title   fiddle   title   fitter   little   title   liter

9. Bob: Bob   Rob   boy   Bab   bob   Don   Dad   Bob
bad   dab

10. form: from   farm   torn   form   tram   horn   form
form   harm

⊛

E. SELECTIVE READING: Cross Out Different Words

■ **Directions:**   Cross out the words and phrases that are different from the word or the phrase on the left. Work quickly.

Example: a book: a book   a ~~look~~   a book   a book   ~~about~~

1. a lot: a box   a lot   a lot   about   a tot   a dog   a lot

2. are common: are common   are coming   are common   or common
are common   are women

3. family name: familiar name   family name   family name
funny name   family name   father's name

4. for women: for women   for women   for woman   four women
for women   from women   for women   to women

5. for example: for examining   for example   an example
four examples   for example   from examples

6. English origin: English origin   English origin   Irish origin
English originally   Spanish origin

7. a nickname: a knickknack   a nickname   a first name   a nickname
   a nickel   the nicknames

8. in fact: in fact   a fact   in fact   or facts   for a fact   in fact
   one fact   in fact

9. not all people: not our people   not all people   for all people
   not all people   a lot of people   not at people

10. most students: most studies   most students   must study
   most students   most students   meet students

(*)

F. SELECTIVE READING: Circle Numbers

■ **Directions:**   Circle the words in each sentence that are numbers. Then write the number in the blank.

   EXAMPLE: There are (twenty-five) students in the class.   _25_

1. The article "NAMES" has seven sections.   _____
2. There are nine paragraphs in the article.   _____
3. This exercise is on page 11.   _____
4. The article "NAMES" begins on page 6.   _____
5. There are twelve exercises in this chapter.   _____
6. Most native English speakers have three names.   _____
7. Some Americans have only two names.   _____
8. It is common for native speakers of Spanish to have four names.   _____

(*)

G. SELECTIVE READING: Underline Examples

■ **Directions:**   Look at the word on the left. Underline the word in the line that is an example of the word on the left.

   EXAMPLE: number: book   pencil   <u>seven</u>   pen
   paper   page

   EXPLANATION: The word *seven* is an example of a number.

1. first name: Johnson   Davis   Elizabeth   Rogers   Baker
2. man's name: Mary   Susan   Kathleen   Margaret   Richard

3. nickname: Arthur   Jennifer   Patty   William   Robert

4. last name: Betty   Taylor   Dave   Debbie   Jim

5. Japanese name: Dumont   Parsons   Sanchez   Tanaka   Bigley

6. title: teacher   student   Mr.   child   woman   man

7. woman's name: Joseph   Steven   Kathy   Bill   Mark   Paul

H. READING CHARTS AND TABLES

■ **(A) Directions:**   Look at Table A. It is a list of the most common last names in the United States and the origins of those names. Then do the exercise.

Table A.   The Ten Most Common Names in the United States in 1974 and Their Origins*

	Rank	Name	Origin
most common - - - - ➤	1	Smith	English, Scottish, Irish
2nd most common - - - - ➤	2	Johnson	English
3rd most common - - - - ➤	3	Williams	Welsh, English
(etc.)	4	Brown	English, Scottish
	5	Jones	Welsh, English
	6	Miller	English
	7	Davis	English, Welsh
	8	Martin	French, English
	9	Anderson	English, Scottish
	10	Wilson	English, Scottish

*Information on ten most common names from: Hook, J.N. *Family Names: How Our Surnames Came to America.* New York: Macmillan, Inc., 1982.

Information on origins of names from: Smith, Elsdon C. *Dictionary of American Family Names.* New York: Harper & Row Publishers, Inc., 1956.

Now look at the following list of names. They are from Table A. They are not in rank order (1, 2, 3 . . .). Put a number by each name to show the rank according to the table.

EXAMPLE: ___8___ Martin   _____ Jones

___5___ Jones   _____ Anderson

___10___ Wilson   _____ Johnson

_____ Davis

_____ Brown

_____ Miller

■ **(B) Directions:** Look at Table B. It is a list of identifying parts of last names. The origins of the parts of names are in alphabetical order (A, B, C, D, E . . .). On the right there are a few example names. After you look at the table, do the exercise.

Table B. Some Identifying Parts of International Last Names

Origin	Identifying Parts	Example Names
Arabic	El-, Al-, -y, -i	El-Ayoubi, Khoury, Zoobi
Armenian	-ian	Akmejian, Hagopian
Chinese	(one syllable)	Chang, Chow, Fu, Kwan
Dutch	van-, -velt	Van Horn, Vandervelt
English	-son, -ton, -er, -ings	Johnson, Winston, Miller, Jennings
French	de-, du-, le-, -eau-	Delacroix, Thibodeaux
German	-berg, -baum, von-, -mann, -sch-	Schiffmann, Newberg, Baumann, von der Tann
Greek	-ulos	Nicopulos, Zatikopoulos
Irish	O'-, Mc-	O'Hara, O'Riley, McMullen
Italian	-ello, -etti, -illo	Morello, Simonetti, Furillo
Japanese	-ta, -da	Fukuda, Nakata
Korean	(one syllable)	Kim, Park
Polish	-ski, -wicz	Kowalski, Janowicz
Russian	-ovich, -ov, -sky	Ivanovich, Kuznetsov, Kaminsky
Scottish	Mac-	MacDuff, MacFarland
Spanish	-ez	Ramirez, Gonzalez
Swedish	-strom-, -quist, -dahl-, -gren	Stromquist, Dahlgren

Now look at the following names. Find the origin of each name by looking at Table B. Circle the identifying part of each name. Write the origin in the blank.

EXAMPLE: Kalinow(ski) _*Polish*_____

1. O'Brien _____

2. Martinez _____

3. Andropoulos _____

4. Rosetti _____

5. DuPree _____

6. Kuroda _____

7. Billings _____

8. Hagstrom _____

⊛
I. PARAPHRASE

Teacher: See the PARAPHRASE exercise, Chapter 2, for further explanation.

■ Directions: Read the pairs of sentences. Is the meaning of each pair (each set of 2 sentences) similar or different? Circle S for *same* or *similar*. Circle D for *different*.

		Same	**Different**
EXAMPLE 1:	a. This exercise is easy. b. This is not a difficult exercise.	(S)	D
EXAMPLE 2:	a. Some sentences have only a few words. b. Some sentences are long.	S	(D)

	Same	**Different**
1. a. The article "NAMES" has an introduction and a conclusion. b. There is an introduction and a conclusion in the article "NAMES."	S	D
2. a. This article has nine paragraphs. b. There are more than nine paragraphs in this article.	S	D
3. a. Many American names do not have an English origin. b. The origin of many American names is not English.	S	D
4. a. Nicknames are common in the United States. b. Some American names do not have nickname forms.	S	D
5. a. Titles such as *Mr., Mrs.,* and *Dr.* are used with last names. b. It is not common to see titles with first names.	S	D

⊛
J. REFERENCE: *it, they, them*

Teacher: It is not necessary at this point to explain in detail the concept of reference. Students need to be able to identify singular and plural nouns and noun phrases, and to understand that *it* is a singular pronoun, and *they* and *them* are plural. They also need to understand the examples, but do not need to explain them. **Note:** a noun phrase is a noun with its determiner and adjectives.

■ (A) Directions: Look at the following groups of words. They are all noun phrases. (See also Chapter 2, LOGICAL WORD GROUPS.) Underline all the nouns in the noun phrases. After each noun phrase, circle **sing.** if the noun is singular. Circle **pl.** if the noun is plural.

	Singular	Plural
EXAMPLE: a book	(sing.)	pl.
some interesting books	sing.	(pl.)

	Singular	Plural
1. a name	sing.	pl.
2. a middle name	sing.	pl.
3. three names	sing.	pl.
4. my name	sing.	pl.
5. your family	sing.	pl.
6. this lesson	sing.	pl.
7. these easy exercises	sing.	pl.
8. the last two examples	sing.	pl.

■ **(B) Directions:** Read the pairs of sentences. What is the meaning of the pronoun in the second sentence? In other words, what does the pronoun **it, they,** or **them** refer to? You will need to find a noun phrase in the first sentence. Study the examples:

EXAMPLE 1: This book has a lot of exercises. It also has articles to read.

It = *this book*

EXAMPLE 2: The exercises in this book are interesting. They are not difficult.

They = *the exercises* (in this book)

EXAMPLE 3: You have two index cards. Your name is on them.

them = *index cards*

We can read "=" as *refers to*: It = this book/It refers to this book.

Now do the exercise. All the pronouns are underlined.

1. First names are popular in the United States. Americans like them.

them = _____

2. This lesson is about names. It gives examples of names in English.

It = _____

3. I have an index card. My name is on <u>it</u>.

it = _____

Think carefully about items 4, 5, and 6.

4. Nicknames are forms of first names. <u>They</u> are common in the United States.

They = _____

5. Titles are words such as *Dr., Mr., Miss,* and *Mrs.* <u>They</u> are used with last names.

They = _____

6. Americans often use first names. For example, many teachers use <u>them</u> with their adult students, as well as with their very young students.

them = _____

K. ACTIVITY: Getting Familiar with Names; Filling in a Chart

■ **Directions:** Look at the chart that follows. Fill it in with more names. Possibilities:

1. Outside class, ask some English speaking people on your school campus to give you some information about their names. You can ask American students, people who work at the school, or other teachers.

2. Look at a telephone book or a campus directory. Fill in the chart with some names. Guess about the origins of the last names if you are not sure. Compare the names on all the charts in class. Ask the teacher to pronounce some of the names. Are some first names the same for males and females?

Chart of Names
(Sex: M = male; F = female)

Sex	First Name	Middle Initial or Name	Last Name	Origin of Last Name
M	John	W.	Davis	English
F	Diane	Marie	Williams	English
F	Miriam	E.	Corneli	Alsatian

Sex	First Name	Middle Initial or Name	Last Name	Origin of Last Name

EXTRA READING

Start Time _____

INTERNATIONAL LAST NAMES:
Look in the Telephone Book!

1   American last names are particularly interesting because they are very in-
2 ternational. Look at some names in the telephone book. You can see that many
3 of the names are not of English origin. In fact, most Americans do not know the
4 origins of the names that they hear and see every day. They need to ask each
5 other "What kind of last name is that?" and "How do you spell your last name?"
6 and "How do you pronounce it?"
7   Of course, names of English origin such as Smith, Johnson, and Davis are
8 very common. You might find one hundred Smiths in the telephone book and
9 only one Kadjevich, one Starzynski, and one Nystrom. But add together the
10 names of non-English origin: one Kadjevich plus one Starzynski plus one Ny-
11 strom plus one. . . . The total will be hundreds, perhaps thousands, of inter-
12 national names. In fact, the number of international last names on just one page
13 of an American telephone book will surprise you! Even more surprising, these
14 names are now *American* names!

TOTAL WORDS: 169   **End Time** _____

Reflection

Think or talk about these questions:

Are there any international names in the telephone books in your country? What
do the names in your telephone books tell you about the people in your country?

EXTRA READING 2

Dr. and Mrs. Jack M. Sorenson Are Pleased to Announce
the Marriage of Their Daughter

Carol Louise
to Mr. James Carl McKay, Jr.
on November 12
in the University Chapel

Reception Follows in the Faculty Club
RSVP

Answer the questions:

1. What do you think this is?
2. Who are Dr. and Mrs. Sorenson?
3. What profession do you think Carol's father has?
4. Who is James McKay?
5. What is happening on November 12?
6. What is Carol's complete name now (= before Nov. 12)?
7. What will her last name be after November 12?
8. What does "Jr." mean?
9. What does "RSVP" mean? (Hint: The letters stand for the French phrase, *Répondez, s'il vous plaît.*)

Teacher: Assist students as needed with the cultural content of this "reading," but encourage them to make inferences on their own or in small groups.

Jamal El-Ayoubi

Chapter 2
Textbooks

PREREADING

Ⓟ Activity: Getting to Know a Book

Materials: Several different books that have titles, tables of contents, chapters, indexes, illustrations, diagrams, photographs; several kinds of markers for underlining purposes.

■ Directions: Each student or small group of students has a book. The books can be different. Do not use this book (***Strategies 1***) yet. Discuss these questions:

1. What is the title of your book?
2. What is the purpose of the title? What does it tell you?
3. Is there a Table of Contents (or just Contents)? Where is it? (Hint: Look in the beginning of the book.)
4. What page(s) is the Table of Contents on? Are these pages numbered with Arabic numerals (1, 2, 3, 4 . . .) or Roman numerals (i, ii, iii, iv . . .)?
5. What kind of information is in the Table of Contents? Are there chapter titles? Chapter headings? Page numbers?

6. Now look at some of the chapters. Are there headings and subheadings in the chapters?

7. Are there illustrations, diagrams, or photographs in the chapters?

8. Look at the back of the book. Is there an Index?

9. What is in the Index? Are there topics and page numbers?

10. Is the Index organized alphabetically (from a to b to c . . .)?

11. Look in the Index. Find a topic that begins with the letter *m* (or another letter). What page is that topic on? Find that topic in the book.

Survey

> **Teacher:**   Help students through the **Survey** and **Scan** sections step by step. They will not learn all the vocabulary in this lesson right away. Assure them that they will have many chances to practice it.

■ **Directions:**   Look at the article ''THIS BOOK.'' Your teacher will ask you some questions about it. Write your answers on a piece of paper or answer orally. You will need to look at the article to find the answers.

1. Look on the left side of the first page of the article. The left side has both information and vocabulary from the article. The article is on the right side of the page. Use the information on the left to help you find the answers to the next questions.

2. What is the **title** of the article? Where is the title?

3. Every paragraph has a number. How many paragraphs are in the article?

4. Are there **headings** in the article? Are there **subheadings?**

5. Copy the title, headings, and subheadings from the article on your paper (or give them orally).

6. Is there a **Summary** section in this article? Where is it?

Scan

■ **Directions:**   Look at the article while you follow these directions from your teacher. Try to find the answers quickly.

1. Find paragraph 3 under the heading SECTIONS AND CHAPTERS. How many parts are in this book? How many sections are in each chapter?

2. How many **footnotes** are in this article? Where are the footnotes? What information do they give you?

3. Look at paragraph 8 under APPENDICES. How many appendices are in *Strategies 1?*

Key Words

1 introduction to the textbook
 articles and exercises
 how to read in English
 practice new vocabulary

2 Contents
   front of the book
   title and contents of each
     chapter
   page numbers

3 two main sections
   several chapters
     four parts

4 Prereading Exercises
 prepare you to read
   topic
   organization
   vocabulary

5 reading article
   title
   illustrations
   headings
   subheadings
   footnotes
   summary

6 reading strategy exercises
 practice how to read
 learn vocabulary

7 two . . . articles
   one topic . . . related
   another topic . . . new
   vocabulary . . . same

8 appendix . . . information at the end
 two appendices

9 index
   back of the book
   list of topics
   alphabetical
   pages

10 Summary

Listen

■ **Directions:** Your teacher will read all or part of the article "THIS BOOK" to you out loud. Follow silently in your book.

Underline

Teacher: (1) Have example markers (colored pens or pencils, wide or narrow felt markers) ready. (2) ⓟ Underline the Key Words in your copy of the text before you do this and other underlining exercises. (3) Demonstrate underlining to students. **Note:** With practice, this exercise will go smoothly, and students will develop their own styles of marking academic material.

■ Directions: Practice underlining.

A. Look at the paragraph on the right. Listen and follow while your teacher reads it out loud.

Key Words	**Paragraph 1**
introduction to the textbook	1 This chapter is an <u>introduction to the textbook</u>, ***Strategies for Readers, Book 1 (Strategies 1)***. ***Strategies 1*** is a book for students of English as a second or foreign language (ESL/EFL). It is for students who already know a little English. This book has many reading <u>articles and exercises.</u> They help you learn <u>how to read in English.</u> They also help you <u>practice new vocabulary.</u> Now let us look at the organization of the book.
articles and exercises	
how to read in English	
practice new vocabulary	

B. Now go back to the beginning of the paragraph. Your teacher will read the paragraph silently. Read silently also. Have your marker ready. Your teacher will read out loud only the underlined Key Words. When you hear them, underline them again by marking over the underlinings.

Teacher: Read the Key Words out loud at the places they would normally occur in a relatively slow silent reading pace. With practice, your students will learn to move their eyes over the material at a similar pace and thus keep up with the underlining.

C. Now go to the beginning of the article. Read silently with your teacher and listen for Key Words. Underline the words that you hear.

Teacher: Practice one paragraph at a time; do not feel obligated to complete the entire article.

Skim

■ Directions: Read quickly the following parts of the article:
   a. the Summary
   b. the headings and subheadings
   c. your underlined Key Words

Predict

■ Directions: Read the statement. It is not complete. It asks you to predict (make a guess about) the main idea in the article. Choose the best answer.

This article is probably going to _____.
a. discuss how to read
b. describe the parts of this textbook
c. explain underlining

SILENT READING

■ Directions: Do a careful reading of the articles in this book *after* you have finished the PREREADING exercises. When you do a careful reading,

1. read silently and
2. read for a purpose.

For example, when you read the article in this chapter, you can read for these purposes:

Purpose 1: Learn the vocabulary in the left margin.
Purpose 2: Be prepared to answer these questions:

1. What kind of information is in the Table of Contents?
2. What are the four parts of each chapter?
3. Look at the list that follows. They are the sections of this textbook. According to the article, which section is first, second, third, and fourth (1st, 2nd, 3rd, 4th)? When you finish reading, put a number (1, 2, 3, 4) by each section in the list to show its place in the book.

_____ Index

_____ Table of Contents

_____ Appendices

_____ Parts and Chapters

**INFORMATION
AND VOCABULARY**

This is the **title**
of the article.

THIS BOOK

ARTICLE

This is a
paragraph number. → 1   This chapter is an introduction to the textbook, ***Strategies for Readers, Book 1 (Strategies 1).*** ***Strategies 1*** is a book for students of English as a second or foreign language (ESL/EFL). It is for students who already know a little English. This book has many articles and exercises. The exercises help you learn how to read in English. They also help you practice new vocabulary. Now let us look at the (**organization**) of the book.

This is paragraph 1.

This word is in
boldface.

This is a **heading.** → TABLE OF CONTENTS

This word is in **boldface.**   2   The Table of Contents is in the front of the book. The Table of Contents is a (**list**) of what is in the book—its contents. The list has the title and contents of each chapter and, on the right, page numbers.
This is paragraph 2.

This is a **heading.** → PARTS AND CHAPTERS

This word is in **boldface.**   3   There are two main sections in this book, called Part 1 and Part 2. Each part has a different (**theme.**) There are several chapters in each main section and each individual chapter has four parts: Prereading Exercises, Main Reading Article, Exercises, and Extra Readings.

This is paragraph 3.

This is a **subheading.** → Prereading Exercises

4   Prereading activities are at the beginning of each chapter. These exercises prepare you to read the article. They: (a) show you something about the topic, (b) show you the organization of the article, and (c) introduce you to some basic vocabulary from the article.

This is paragraph 4.

This is a **subheading.** ─────────► Article

This is paragraph 5.   5   The second (2nd) part of each chapter is the reading article. Each article has a title and some diagrams, illustrations, or photographs. Most of the articles have (**headings**) at the beginning of main sections, some (**subheadings,**) and some (**footnotes**[1]) to help you with vocabulary or ideas. Some articles have a Summary section at the end. The Summary gives the main ideas of the article in a few sentences.

These words are in **boldface.**

This is a **footnote number.** Look for footnote 1 at the bottom of this page.

This is a **subheading.** ─────────► Exercises

This is paragraph 6.   6   The third (3rd) part of each chapter is Reading Strategy Exercises. There are ten to sixteen (10–16) exercises in each chapter, and each exercise is different. The vocabulary in the exercises is from the reading article. In general, the reading exercises help you practice how to read and help you learn vocabulary.

This is a **subheading.** ─────────► Extra Readings

This is paragraph 7.   7   The last part of each chapter consists of two short reading articles. One topic is related to the topic of the main reading article. Another topic is new. A lot of the vocabulary is the same in all the readings in each chapter.

This is a **heading.** ─────────► APPENDICES

This word is in **boldface.**   8   An (**appendix**) is extra information at the end of a book. In ***Strategies 1,*** there are two appendices. Appendix 1 will help you calculate your reading rate. Appendix 2 is a list of key words from the Key Words list in each chapter. Appendices are useful, but they are (*not included in all books.*)

This is paragraph 8.

These words are in *italics.*

This is a **heading.** ─────────► INDEX

This is paragraph 9.   9   The Index is at the very back of the book. It has a list of topics and subjects in alphabetical order, from a to z. The Index also shows which pages of the book cover each topic.

This is footnote 1.

---

[1]footnotes (n, C, p1) = notes at the bottom of a page that explain a word or an idea in the article. Each footnote has a number.

This is a **footnote number.**

This is a **heading.**

SUMMARY[2]

10   This article describes the book, ***Strategies for Readers, Book 1.*** The book is divided into three main sections: (1) Table of Contents, (2) Parts and Chapters, and (3) Appendices and Index. Each chapter has four parts: Prereading Exercises, Main Reading Article, Exercises, and Extra Readings.

This is paragraph 10. It is the **summary** of the article.

This is footnote 2.

[2]summary (n, C) = the main ideas of the article, usually in one or two statements.

EXERCISES

A. COMPREHENSION CHECK: True or False

■ Directions: Read the statements about the article. Write T after the statements that are true. Write F after the statements that are false.

1. This article explains the organization of this textbook.   _____

2. The two main parts of this book are divided into Chapters.   _____

3. The Table of Contents is the same as a Chapter.   _____

4. Every Chapter has two Extra Readings.   _____

5. This article, "THIS BOOK," does not have a Summary section.   _____

6. There are ten footnotes in this article.   _____

B. COMPREHENSION CHECK: Multiple Choice

■ Directions: Choose the best answer. Write the letter in the blank.

1. In general, this article _____.
   a. describes the parts of the book
   b. describes one chapter
   c. describes footnotes

2. The Table of Contents is _____.
   a. a list of vocabulary
   b. a list of chapter titles
   c. a list of answers

3. Each chapter in this book has ———— parts.
   a. five
   b. three
   c. four

4. A summary comes ———— of a chapter.
   a. at the beginning
   b. in the middle
   c. at the end

5. The Appendix is ———— the book.
   a. in the front of
   b. in the back of
   c. not in

6. Boldface letters are ———— than other letters.
   a. larger
   b. smaller
   c. heavier and blacker

(✷)

C. COMPREHENSION CHECK: Answer

■ **Directions:**   Go back to the questions under Purpose 2 in the SILENT READING section. Answer those questions.

D. SELECTIVE READING: Underline Same Words

■ **Directions:**   Look at the word on the left. Underline the same word(s) in the line. Work as quickly as possible.

   EXAMPLE: exercise: excellent   example   <u>exercise</u>   exchange

1. article: articulate   article   artichoke   artifice   article
   artificial

2. chapter: chapel   charcoal   charity   chapter   shatter   sharper

3. purpose: purpose   purchase   purpose   porpoise   purport
   pursue

4. organization: originate   organize   organizing   organization
   organized

5. heading: headline   heading   heading   reading   heating
   beating

6. footnote: foothill   foothold   footnote   footrace   footnote
footman

7. summary: summary   summarily   summarize   summery
summary   summary

8. diagram: diagnose   diadem   diagonal   diagram   dialogue
diagram

9. vocabulary: vocalize   vocabulary   constabulary   vocation
vocabulary   vocalization

10. paragraph: paradox   paragraph   parallel   paragraph   parakeet
paragraph

E. SELECTIVE READING: Cross Out Different Phrases

■ **Directions:**   Look at the group of words on the left. Cross out the groups of words in the lines that are different. Work as quickly as possible.

EXAMPLE: on the right: on the right   on the right   in the night
on the sight   in the light   in the right
on the right   on the right

1. four parts: four parts   for parts   four parts   four pants   for backs
four barbs   four parts   for barter   four parts

2. page number: paid number   page number   page numeral
page numbered   page number   page number
pack number   part number

3. how to read: how to lead   how to read   how to read   who to read
slow to read   how to deal   how to read   show to read

4. the main idea: the main idea   the same idea   the main idea
a main idea   the rain idea   the main ideal
the main idea   the main idea

5. a short section: a short session   a short section   a short section
a shore section   a sure section   a short section
a shored section

6. is related to: is related to   as related to   is related by   is related to
is berated by   is related to   is relative to   is belated for

7. in the index: in the index   in the index   in an index   in the indexes
on the index   in the inbox   is indeed   in the index

F. SELECTIVE READING: Cross Out Unrelated Word

■ **Directions:** Look at the word on the left. Then cross out the word in the line that does not belong with it. Work as quickly as possible.

EXAMPLE: Mary: Tom   Bob   Mike   ~~book~~   Susan   Bill

EXPLANATION: The word on the left (Mary) is a name. The word *book* is not a name. All the other words are names.

1. first: fourth   second   fifth   name   third   sixth
2. English: Irish   Japanese   Spanish   John   Italian   Arabic
3. chapter: unit   title   contents   index   number   exercises
4. Mr.:   Miss   Ms.   married   Dr.   Prof.   Mrs.
5. diagram: photograph   illustration   picture   paragraph
6. noun: adjective   sentence   adverb   verb   preposition
7. listen: speak   read   answer   eat   write   ask
8. usually: read   sometimes   often   always   never
9. in: page   on   about   for   to   at   with
10. first name: nickname   middle name   family name   American name

⊛

G. LOGICAL WORD GROUPS

EXPLANATION: Reading is easier if you can identify **logical word groups.** A logical word group is a group of words that go together in a grammatical way. Here are some examples:

1. Noun Phrases
   a book
   your first name
   these difficult exercises

2. Predicates
   is easy
   are students
   have five brothers and sisters

3. Prepositional Phrases
   on the left
   in the margin
   about the topic

Now read this sentence:

A logical word group is a group of words that go together in a grammatical way.

This sentence is made up of two main logical word groups:

A logical word group   (noun phrase)
is a group of words that go together in a logical way   (predicate)

The predicate is also made up of several logical word groups:*

is a group of words   (verb phrase)
that go together   (adjective clause)
in a logical way   (prepositional phrase)

Practice: Read the groups of words from the example sentence. Circle (YES) if the groups are logical and grammatical. Circle (NO) if they are not logical groups. Can you explain your answers?

		Logical Word Group?	
1.	A logical	YES	NO
2.	is a group	YES	NO
3.	go together	YES	NO
4.	group of	YES	NO
5.	in a	YES	NO
6.	a logical way	YES	NO

■ Directions: Read the following paragraph from the article. It is written in logical word groups in two ways: (a) vertically (up and down); and (b) horizontally (across). In a and b you can see the logical word groups easily and adjust your reading to them. Then read the same paragraph with normal spacing (c). Can you still read in logical word groups?

a. Vertical

The Prereading Exercises
are at the beginning
of each chapter.
These exercises
prepare you
to read the article.
They

*Other divisions and labelings are possible.

(a) show you something
about the topic,
(b) show you the organization
of the article, and
(c) introduce you
to some basic vocabulary
from the article.

b. Horizontal

The Prereading Exercises   are at the beginning   of each chapter.   These exercises   prepare you   to read the article.   They   (a) show you something
about the topic,   (b) show you the organization   of the article, and   (c) introduce
you   to some basic vocabulary   from the article.

c. Normal Spacing

The Prereading Exercises are at the beginning of each chapter. These exercises
prepare you to read the article. They (a) show you something about the topic, (b) show
you the organization of the article, and (c) introduce you to some basic vocabulary from
the article.

H. ORDER: Alphabetical

■ **Directions:**   Put the words in alphabetical order (a, b, c, d . . .) by putting a number
next to each word. You will need to look at the first letter of each word.

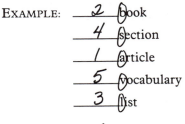

EXAMPLE: _2_ book
_4_ section
_1_ article
_5_ vocabulary
_3_ list

1. _____ paragraph

_____ sentence

_____ exercise

_____ diagram

_____ number

_____ part

_____ unit

_____ chapter

2. _____ Tanigawa

_____ Bailey

_____ Martinez

_____ Dennis

_____ Wong

_____ Page

_____ Haffar

3. Arrange the names of the students in your class alphabetically. Use index cards or write the names on the blackboard.

I.   REFERENCE: *it, they, them*

■ **Directions:**   Read the sentences. The first sentence has one or two noun phrases. The second sentence has one or two pronouns (*it, they, them*). The underlined pronouns refer to a noun phrase in the first sentence. Write the noun phrase in the blank.

EXAMPLE: This textbook has a Table of Contents. It has an Index, too.

It =   *This textbook*

1. This book is a reading text. It is for students who know a little English.

It = _____

2. The chapters have four parts. They are: Prereading Exercises, Reading Article, Exercises, and Extra Readings.

They = _____

3. The Prereading Exercises prepare you to read the article. They show you something about the topic.

They = _____

4. The Prereading Exercises give you some information about the article. Do them before you read it.

them = _____

it = _____

5. The Table of Contents is a list. You can use it to find chapter titles and page numbers.

it = _____

6. The footnotes give useful information or explanations. They are at the bottom of the page.

They = _____

7. A summary gives the main ideas of an article. It gives them in one or two sentences.

It = _____

them = _____

J. PARAPHRASE

EXPLANATION: A **paraphrase** is a different way to say the same thing. In other words, it is a new sentence (different words, different grammar) with the same or similar meaning as an original sentence.

> EXAMPLE: (original sentence) This textbook has many exercises.
> (paraphrase) There are many exercises in this textbook.

■ Directions: Now read the pairs of sentences. Is the meaning of the two sentences similar or different? Circle S if the meaning is the same or similar. Circle D if the meaning is different. (See the PARAPHRASE exercise in Chapter 1 for examples.)

	Same	**Different**
1. a. There are six chapters in the book. b. The book has six chapters.	S	D
2. a. Each article has illustrations or photographs. b. Illustrations and photographs contain useful information.	S	D
3. a. It is important to learn vocabulary. b. Learning vocabulary is important.	S	D
4. a. The third part of each chapter is reading strategy exercises. b. Section three of each chapter contains reading strategy exercises.	S	D
5. a. Extra readings at the end of each chapter give more reading and vocabulary practice. b. Reading is a good way to practice vocabulary.	S	D
6. a. Some of the pairs of sentences in this exercise have the same meaning. b. Two sentences with different meanings are not examples of paraphrase.	S	D
7. a. The topics in an index are organized alphabetically. b. The list of subjects in an index is in alphabetical order—from a to z.	S	D
8. a. Key words are the most important words in a sentence. b. It is important to recognize key words in a sentence.	S	D

(✱)

K. OUTLINING

■ Directions: Read the example outline. Then answer the questions as best you can.

OUTLINE

I. Introductory paragraph	(1)
II. Table of contents	( )
A. List	( )
B. Chapter title and page numbers	( )
III. Parts and chapters	( )
A. Two main sections	( )
B. Several chapters	( )
C. Four parts in each chapter	( )
1. Prereading exercises	( )
2. Main reading article	( )
3. Exercises	( )
4. Extra readings	( )
D. Prereading exercises	( )
1. Topic	( )
2. Organization	( )
3. Basic vocabulary	( )
E. Main reading article	( )
1. Illustrations	( )
2. Headings, subheadings, footnotes	( )
F. Exercises	( )
1. 10 to 16	( )
2. Reading and vocabulary practice	( )
G. Extra readings	( )
1. Short articles	( )

    2. Related topic   (   )

    3. New topic   (   )

  IV. Appendices   (   )

   V. Index   (   )

  VI. Summary   (   )

1. An outline is an organized presentation of important ideas or topics. This outline is from a reading article in your book. What article is it from?

2. Compare the reading article with the outline. What paragraph is each item in the outline from? Write the paragraph number in the parentheses ( ) after each item. The first one is done for you.

3. This outline has three (3) kinds of letters and numbers to help organize the ideas in the reading article. Can you give examples of each kind?

4. Read the list of letter and number types in a typical outline. Check (✔) the types that you see in this outline and give an example of each one.

(   ) Roman numerals   Example: _____

(   ) Arabic numerals   Example: _____

(   ) Upper case (capital) letters   Example: _____

(   ) Lower case (small) letters   Example: _____

L. ACTIVITY: Looking at Books and Magazines from Your Country

■ **Directions:** From home, bring a book or magazine to class that is written in your native language. *Briefly,* explain your book or magazine to the class. Be sure to answer the following questions:

1. What kind of book or magazine is it? Textbook? History? Novel or stories? Sports? Home and garden? Other?

2. How is the book or magazine organized? Is there a table of contents or an index? Are there chapters or sections? Titles, headings, and subheadings? Pictures? If there are pictures, what kind are they? Photographs? Drawings? If you have a magazine, are there advertisements?

3. What topics are there in your book or magazine?

4. How is your book or magazine different from American ones?

    When everyone is finished talking, discuss in class what your favorite reading material is. Do the students in your class enjoy reading different things?

EXTRA READING

Start Time _____

THE HELPFUL FEATURES OF TEXTBOOKS

1   Textbooks are books that students use in school. Students at all levels and
2   in all kinds of schools use textbooks. The purpose of textbooks is to help us
3   learn. Therefore, all textbooks have certain features in common—features that
4   help us find and understand the information in them. For example, textbooks
5   have tables of contents at the beginning. The tables of contents list the chapter
6   titles, the parts of the chapters, and the page numbers of the parts. Textbooks
7   help us understand information in another way: They divide the information
8   into chapters, lessons, or units. These sections are divided again, into smaller
9   parts with headings and subheadings. Finally, most textbooks have an index at
10 the back of the book. The index lists all the topics in the book in alphabetical
11 order, and gives their page numbers. All of these features—tables of contents,
12 chapters and chapter divisions, and indexes—help us find and understand the
13 information in textbooks quickly and efficiently.

TOTAL WORDS: 161   **End Time** _____

Reflection

Think or talk about these questions:

Think about the textbooks that you use in the schools in your country. Do they have the same features as the textbooks that are described in this reading? Are the parts organized in the same way or in a different order? What other features of textbooks can help you find and understand information?

EXTRA READING 2

CONTENTS

Answer the questions:

1. What do you think this is?
2. What kind of book is it from?
3. Can you think of a good title for this book?
4. What will you find on page 10?
5. What will you find on page 21?
6. What kind of information do you think will be in Chapter 4?

Part 2
Things

The word *thing* is very general. A thing can be an object on your desk, a piece of furniture, a utensil like a fork or a knife, a can or a bottle, an article of clothing like a sweater or a coat, and even a rock or a piece of wood. In other words, a thing can be almost any object that you can see, touch, or pick up. The articles in Part 2 are about things—things that are around you, things that you see every day. There is a lot of vocabulary in this part. Most of the vocabulary consists of nouns—words that name things. In addition to learning the English words for familiar things around you, you will continue developing your reading skills.

Now, think about these questions:

> What things are around me? What things do I see, use, and touch every day?

Teacher: The use of real objects throughout this unit can make these lessons about very familiar objects come alive. For added motivation, ask your students to bring a few of their own things to class. **Note:** Although the topic of each reading article is different, the rhetorical structure of the articles is similar. It is hoped that this rather narrow rhetorical focus will facilitate comprehension.

Chapter 3
Classrooms

Patricia Hall

PREREADING

Activity: Getting Familiar with the Things in Your Classroom

Materials: None, other than typical classroom furniture and objects.

- Directions:

Teacher: Time this activity, especially if it is a contest or a game. You will function as a vocabulary resource person. Circulate quickly to each group as needed. Review directions with the class before dividing into small groups.

Divide the class into small groups (or two teams for a game). Follow these steps. You will have (10) minutes.

1. Look around your classroom. What things do you see? In your group, make a list on a piece of paper of everything you can find in the room. To learn new vocabulary, (a) first ask everyone in your group. (b) If nobody knows the correct English word, ask your teacher. (c) If your teacher is busy with another group, use your dictionary.

2. At the end of (10) minutes, compare lists. Which group (or team) has the most items? Does each group have the same items? Which items are different?

3. Make a master list (one combined list) on the blackboard. Discuss how you might categorize all the items (*furniture, things to write with, things on the wall, large or small objects*).

4. Which items on the master list are **countable nouns** (C) and which are **uncountable nouns** (U)? Mark each item with a C or a U.*

> EXAMPLE: a chair, some chairs = *C*
>
> furniture = *U*

Survey

■ Directions: Look at the article "CLASSROOMS." Follow these directions from your teacher. Answer orally or in writing.

1. What are the title and headings in this article? Copy them on your paper (or give them orally).

2. How many illustrations (figures) are there in this article (Figure 1, Figure 2 . . .)?

3. What is the subject of the illustrations? Is it the *objects* in the classroom? The *arrangement of furniture* in classrooms? *Similarities* among classrooms? Choose one.

Scan

■ Directions: Continue looking at the article. Follow these directions from your teacher. Write your answers. Work quickly. Do not try to read every word.

1. How many footnotes are in this article?

2. In the section SIMILARITIES, what words have a footnote number?

3. In the section DIFFERENCES, look at Figures 1, 2, 3. What is the **title** of each figure?

4. In the section DIFFERENCES, look at paragraph 9. This paragraph talks about the **atmosphere** in classrooms. It mentions three kinds of **lighting.** What are they?

---

*Most uncountable nouns in fact have a plural form, but with a change of meaning: paper (U); papers (C) = *kinds* of paper. Some uncountable nouns are *only* plural: clothes, glasses (= spectacles), scissors, pants.

5. Look at paragraph 12 in the section CONCLUSION. What is the meaning of "a great deal of"?

Key Words

1 classrooms
   different in some ways
   also similar
2 similarities
   chairs or desks
   desk or lectern
3 blackboard
   chalk
   erasers
4 books, paper, pencils, and pens
5 also many differences
6 first
   arrangement of furniture
      rows
      semicircle
      circle
7 second
   other kinds of furniture
      shelves
      cupboards or closets
      tables
8 third
   different objects
      chalk
      erasers

9 finally
   atmosphere
      large
      small
      lighting
      color
      pictures and maps
10 Why are there differences?
11 one reason for differences
   different purposes
      kind of class
      age of the students
12 another reason
   money
13 third reason
   cultural
   different ideas influence . . .
      classrooms
14 main purpose . . . the same
   students and teachers . . . come together

Listen

■ Directions: Listen while your teacher reads out loud all or part of the article "CLASSROOMS." Follow silently in your book.

Underline

(See the **Underline** sections in Chapters 1 and 2 for explanation.)

■ Directions: Go to the beginning of the article "CLASSROOMS." Your teacher will read the article with you silently and will speak out loud only the Key Words. Underline the Key Words as you hear them.

Skim

■ **Directions:**   Now skim the entire article.

a. Read paragraph 1, INTRODUCTION.
b. Read the headings in the article and look at the illustrations again.
c. Read your underlined Key Words.

Predict

■ **Directions:**   Choose the best answer.

The article "CLASSROOMS" is going to discuss _____.
a. the kinds of furniture in American and British classrooms
b. different kinds of teaching and learning
c. how classrooms in the world are similar and different

SILENT READING

■ **Directions:**   Now read the article "CLASSROOMS" carefully, but as quickly as you can. Be prepared to think about these questions when you finish reading:

1. What are classrooms in your country like? (What are their characteristics?)
2. Can you compare the classrooms in your country with the information in each paragraph of the article?

CLASSROOMS

INTRODUCTION

1   Classrooms exist in every country of the world. They are rooms in schools—very important rooms. In classrooms, students and teachers meet together, and the activities of teaching and learning take place. Each country has different ideas about teaching and learning. Therefore, classrooms are probably different in some ways from country to country. But classrooms everywhere are also similar in some ways. They have certain things in common.

SIMILARITIES

2   What **similarities** can we find among classrooms? Classrooms are places for students and teachers to meet. Classrooms, therefore, have chairs or desks for the students, and a desk or lectern[1] for the teacher. These pieces of furniture are basic.

---

[1] a lectern (n, C) = a piece of furniture which a teacher or speaker stands behind.

3   Most classrooms have a blackboard[2] in front of the room. Teachers and students use blackboards in many different ways, but in general, important information is written on blackboards. Teachers and students write on blackboards with chalk because chalk is easy to erase. Therefore, in addition to chalk, you can find erasers in all classrooms with blackboards. Blackboards are extremely useful in classrooms for just this reason: We can use them, erase them, and use them again.

4   Finally, classrooms all over the world have similar objects in them. For example, books, paper, pencils, and pens are very common classroom objects. Both teachers and students use these things every day.

DIFFERENCES

5   There are also many **differences** among classrooms, not just from country to country and school to school, but from classroom to classroom. Let us look at a few of the differences we might find among classrooms.

6   First, the basic arrangement of furniture may be different. In most classrooms, the students' chairs are in rows and the teacher's desk or table is in front of the room (Figure 1). In other classrooms, for example in classrooms for small classes of ten or fifteen students, the chairs may be in a semicircle (Figure 2), or perhaps even in a closed circle (Figure 3).

7   Second, some classrooms have other kinds of furniture, in addition to students' chairs and a teacher's desk. Some examples of other pieces of furniture

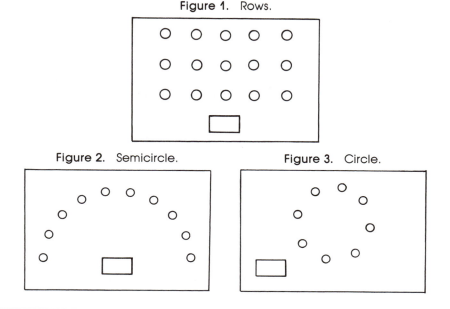

Figure 1. Rows.

Figure 2. Semicircle.   Figure 3. Circle.

---

[2]A blackboard is also called a *chalkboard*.

are shelves, cupboards or closets, and large round,[3] rectangular,[4] or square[5] tables where several students can work.

8   Third, classrooms have different objects in them. Most classrooms have chalk and erasers for the blackboard. But some classrooms also have books, magazines, and newspapers on shelves or on tables. Classrooms for children often have games and toys in them, perhaps on shelves or in cupboards and closets. Many classrooms for children now have computers, too. Language classrooms may have language games, maps, pictures, posters, cassette recorders, video equipment, and computers. Science classrooms have equipment for science demonstrations and experiments.

9   Finally, the atmosphere in classrooms is different. The atmosphere of a room is difficult to describe, because many factors[6] influence it. For example, the size of a room influences the atmosphere. Very large classrooms have a different feeling from very small classrooms. In other words, large and small classrooms have different atmospheres. Lighting is another factor that influences the atmosphere of a room. Lighting can be natural (from windows), electric, or fluorescent. Each kind of lighting creates a different atmosphere. Color and pattern influence the atmosphere of a room, too. A classroom with bare white walls is very different from a classroom with brightly colored walls. Many pictures and maps on the walls change the atmosphere again.

CONCLUSION: WHY ARE THERE DIFFERENCES?

10   Classrooms throughout the world are both similar and different. The similarities are easy to understand. But why are there differences?

11   Perhaps one reason for differences among classrooms is that classes have different specific purposes. In other words, teachers and students do different things in classrooms, depending on the kind of class (history, foreign language, science) and on the age of the students (children, teenagers, adults).

12   Another reason for differences among classrooms may be money. Each school has a different budget.[7] Some schools have a great deal of[8] money, and some schools have very little money. The classrooms in these schools are, of course, very different.

13   A third reason for differences among classrooms is cultural. Ideas about education are different throughout the world. These different ideas influence the

---

[3]round (adj) = ◯

[4]rectangular (adj) = ▭

[5]square (adj) = ▢

[6]factors (n, C, pl) = things or situations that influence something else

[7]a budget (n, C) = a plan for spending money

[8]a great deal of = a lot of

design, plan, and arrangement of classrooms. Different ideas about teaching and learning also influence the kinds of things you can find in classrooms.

14   Classrooms all over the world are places where many different kinds of teaching and learning take place. But the main purpose of classrooms everywhere is the same. That purpose is to provide a location[9] for students and teachers to come together, to think, to study, to teach, and to learn.

EXERCISES

A. COMPREHENSION CHECK: Outlining; Using an Outline for Information

> **Teacher:** If your students did not do the outlining exercise in Chapter 2, do this outline with them on the blackboard.

■ **(A) Directions:** Complete the outline with information from the article.

  I. Introduction

 II. Similarities

    A. Chairs and desks

    B.

    C.

III. Differences

    A. Arrangement of furniture

       1. Rows

       2.

       3.

    B.

    C.

    D.

 IV. Conclusion

Can you find examples for III B, C, and D? What number or letter type do you need to use with these examples?

---

[9]a location (n, C) = a place

■ (B) Directions: Read the questions from the SILENT READING section (before the article) again. Can you answer them from your own knowledge and from the outline?

B.   COMPREHENSION CHECK: True or False

■ **Directions:**   Write T after the statements that are true according to the article. Write F after the statements that are false.

1. A blackboard and a chalkboard are the same thing.   _____

2. The most common arrangement of chairs in a classroom is a circle.   _____

3. Some small classes have the chairs in a semicircle.   _____

4. It is possible to find cassette recorders and computers in some language classrooms.   _____

5. Lighting influences the atmosphere of a room.   _____

6. Ideas about teaching and learning are the same throughout the world.   _____

C.   COMPREHENSION CHECK: Multiple Choice

■ **Directions:**   Choose the best answer. Write the letter in the blank.

1. You can find _____ in most classrooms.
   a. cupboards   c. a blackboard
   b. computers   d. games

2. A semicircular arrangement of chairs is good for a _____ class.
   a. large   c. male
   b. female   d. small

3. Size, color, and light can influence the _____ of a classroom.
   a. atmosphere   c. furniture
   b. temperature   d. windows

4. One reason why classrooms are different is _____.
   a. some classrooms are large
   b. there are different kinds of classes in them
   c. chairs are in rows or in semicircles
   d. the books are different

5. This article is about _____.
   a. the arrangement of chairs
   b. classroom atmosphere
   c. classroom similarities and differences
   d. classroom objects

D. SELECTIVE READING: Cross Out Unrelated Word

- **Directions:** Read the line of words. One word in each line does not belong with the other words. Cross it out. Work as quickly as possible.

    EXAMPLE: three   nine   seven   ~~white~~   two   four

    EXPLANATION: *White* is a color. All the other words are numbers.

1. chair   desk   table   lectern   window   shelf
2. teach   pencil   write   read   learn   study   think
3. similar   round   circular   rectangular   square
4. magazines   books   pencils   newspapers   dictionaries
5. second   two   third   first   fifth   fourth   last
6. white   red   yellow   blue   green   large   brown
7. teacher   man   professor   doctor   dentist   lawyer
8. games   toys   pictures   students   maps   cassettes
9. Miss   teacher   Dr.   Mrs.   Mr.   Ms.   Prof.

E. SELECTIVE READING: Underline Examples

- **Directions:** Look at the word on the left. Then read the line of words. Some of the words in the line are examples of the word on the left. Underline the examples. Work quickly.

    EXAMPLE: room: number   <u>classroom</u>   <u>restroom</u>   <u>office</u>   book

    EXPLANATION: *Classrooms, restrooms,* and *offices* are kinds of rooms.

1. furniture: desk   pencil   chair   blackboard   chalk
2. shapes: classroom   square   round   big   rectangular   white
3. equipment: student   cassette recorder   computer   teacher   lesson
4. lighting: lectern   electric   shelf   cupboard   fluorescent
5. book: map   magazine   textbook   dictionary   eraser
6. country: city   Japan   English   Johnson   Mexico   Egypt
7. English name: Smith   McDonald   Davis   Sanchez   Tekawa
    Li

F. ORDER: Alphabetical

■ **(A) Directions:**   Look at the list of words. They are in random order (not organized). Rewrite them in alphabetical order. Notice that four words begin with the same letter (c).

Random Order	Alphabetical Order
eraser	
chalk	
paper	
blackboard	
shelf	
closet	
game	
cassette	
row	
table	
atmosphere	
computer	

■ **(B) Directions:**   Look at the list of words. All of them begin with the same letter. Rewrite the list in alphabetical order by looking at the second (or third) letter in each word.

Random Order	Alphabetical Order
book	
blackboard	
big	
Betty	
Bob	
basic	
best	
beginning	

Ⓟ **(C) Dictionary Work**

Teacher: If students do not have English-English dictionaries, bring several to class and have students in small groups take turns. You can do this exercise as a game (a "Dictionary Race") in which speed in locating words is the factor that wins points. Add or change words as needed.

■ **Directions:** You will need an English-English dictionary for this exercise. As you know, dictionaries are organized alphabetically. Find the following words as quickly as possible:

> rectangle
> middle
> write
> organization
> question
> through

✱

G. ORDER: Ordinal Numbers

■ **Directions:** Look at the lists of ordinal numbers (= numbers that show order). Match the number form with the ordinal form. Draw a line to connect the two forms. Then draw a line from the ordinal word form to the matching cardinal word form (= the word that names the number). Follow the example that is done: 1st ⟶ first ⟶ one.

Number Form	Ordinal Word Form	Cardinal Word Form
2nd	ninth	five
4th	third	nine
9th	tenth	one
5th	fourth	six
1st	sixth	two
3rd	second	ten
10th	fifth	four
6th	first	three

Note: Study carefully the spelling of both forms.

(*)

H. ORDER: Sequential

■ **(A) Directions:**   Read the list of sentences. They are in random order (= not organized). Put a number (1, 2, 3, 4, 5) in front of each sentence to show the correct sequence.

_____   Third, some classrooms have a lot of equipment in them.

_____   First, the arrangement of chairs is often different.

_____   Finally, classrooms have different atmospheres.

_____   Let us look at some differences among classrooms.

_____   Second, some classrooms have different kinds of furniture.

■ **(B) Directions:**   Discuss these questions in class:

1. What words in part A show sequential order? Make a list.
2. Can you think of other words that show sequential order? What are they?

(*)

I. AGREE/DISAGREE

EXPLANATION: Some answers and ideas are not right or wrong—they depend on your opinion. In other words, you can **agree** or **disagree** with an answer or idea.

> EXAMPLE: Do you agree (A) or disagree (D) with the following statement? Circle A or D, according to your opinion.

> **Large classes** (= classes with many students) **are good.**

> A   D

We cannot say that this statement is true or false. It is "true" for some people in some situations. It is "false" for other people in other situations. If we add more information, perhaps more people will have the same answer (will agree with each other):

Large foreign language classes are good.

A   D

Many people now will probably circle D. Can you think why? But some people might agree with the statement, and have reasons for agreeing.

■ **Directions:** Read the statements. Circle A if you agree. Circle D if you disagree. Discuss your answers in class.

	Agree	Disagree
1. It is nice to have a lot of windows in a classroom.	A	D
2. The best place for the teacher to stand is in front of the class and behind a desk, table, or lectern.	A	D
3. The best arrangement for chairs in a classroom is in rows.	A	D
4. Books, magazines, newspapers, games, pictures, and maps are necessary objects in a foreign language class.	A	D
5. Bright colors (blue, red, yellow, green . . .) in a classroom create a nice atmosphere for studying.	A	D
6. The white light of fluorescent lighting is better in classrooms than the yellow light of regular electric lighting.	A	D

⊛

J. GUESS

EXPLANATION: There are several good ways to find the meaning of a new word. One way is to look in a dictionary. Another way is to ask someone. A third way is to **guess.** It is not always possible to guess the meaning of a word, however. For example, in this sentence,

The cyclamen is beautiful.

it is not possible to guess the meaning of *cyclamen*. The other words in the sentence do not give us enough information. But in this sentence,

There are many beautiful cyclamens in the garden.

we can make a very general guess about cyclamens: They are probably plants. The word *garden*, an easier word than cyclamen, gives us that information. In the next sentence,

The beautiful cylcamens add a lot of color to the garden.

we can probably make a better guess: Cyclamens are probably plants with colorful flowers. The words *garden* and *color* help us make this guess.

Is it necessary to know the exact meaning (the translation) of the word *cyclamen?* Probably not. It is enough to know that a cyclamen is a plant with flowers.

IMPORTANT: In many cases you do not need to know the exact meaning of a word. A general meaning is often good enough. Sometimes it is possible to guess at general meanings. Let's practice this.

■ Directions: Read the sentences. One word in each sentence is underlined. Then read the three possible choices for the general meaning of the underlined word. Use the other words in the sentence to help you guess the general meaning.

EXAMPLE: The proprietor opened the door.

A *proprietor* is probably _____.
a. a plant   b. an animal   c. a person

The best guess is c, a person. The words *opened the door* helped us guess: Can a plant open a door? No. Can an animal open a door? Possibly yes, in some special cases. Can a person open a door? Yes, of course. Now continue this exercise.

1. The preface is in the front of a book.

A preface is probably _____.
a. a person
b. a section in a book
c. a machine
What words in the sentence helped you guess?

2. The author doesn't use his middle name.

An author is probably _____.
a. an animal
b. a book
c. a person
What words in the sentence helped you guess?

3. The author writes a new book every year.

An author is probably _____.
a. a person who writes books
b. a person who teaches
c. a person who works in a restaurant
What words in the sentence helped you guess?

4. There is a wastebasket in the classroom.

A wastebasket is probably _____.
a. a person
b. a table
c. It is not possible to guess.
What words in the sentence helped you guess?

5. There is a small plastic wastebasket in the corner of the classroom.

A wastebasket is probably _____.

a. a small table
b. some kind of object
c. either a or b
What words in the sentence helped you guess?

6. The plastic <u>wastebasket</u> in the classroom is full of old papers and other trash.

   A wastebasket is probably _____.
   a. a table
   b. a container for trash
   c. a chair
   What words in the sentence helped you guess?

7. <u>Tables</u> are useful.   (Be careful!)

   A table is probably _____.
   a. a kind of furniture
   b. a part of a book
   c. It is not possible to guess.
   What words in the sentence helped you guess?

8. The <u>tables</u> in the book are useful.

   A table is probably _____.
   a. a picture of a kind of furniture
   b. a part of a book
   c. either a or b
   What words in the sentence helped you guess?

9. The <u>table</u> in the back of the dictionary shows common first names in alphabetical order.

   A table is probably _____.
   a. a kind of furniture
   b. an organized list in a book
   c. either a or b
   What words in the sentence helped you guess?

(*)
K. VOCABULARY STUDY

Teacher: Make sure that at least every third student has an English-English dictionary. (If students haven't done so already, now is the time for them to buy small pocket dictionaries.) In this exercise, students will be learning to identify how their dictionaries label parts of speech. (See VOCABULARY STUDY, Chapter 6, for practice at locating appropriate meanings.) If students choose words that are labeled as more than one part of speech, ask how the words are used in the article.

■ **Directions:** Choose three (or more) words from the reading article that you would like to look up in the dictionary. Write them in the first column on the left.

Word	**Part of Speech**	**Abbreviation in My Dictionary**
_____	_____	_____
_____	_____	_____
_____	_____	_____
(column 1)	**(column 2)**	**(column 3)**

Now look up each word in your English-English dictionary. Find the abbreviation (usually one to three letters) that shows the part of speech of each word. Write the full name of the part of speech in the second column. Then write your dictionary's abbreviation for the part of speech in the third column. (**Note:** Some abbreviations are a little different from dictionary to dictionary.)

EXAMPLES:	**Word**	**Part of Speech**	**Abbreviation**
	through	preposition	prep.
	book	noun	n.
	logical	adjective	adj.
	be	verb	vb.

L. UNDERLINING PRACTICE

■ **Directions:** The paragraph that follows is about an imaginary language school. On the left, some key words from the paragraph are in parentheses. As you read the paragraph, underline the words that are the same as the words on the left. Work quickly. The first underlining is done for you.

(small classes)
(three levels)

(beginning intermediate advanced)
(fifteen chairs)
(television video)
(books games cassette)

(walls)
(maps posters)
(large windows)
(atmosphere)
(pleasant)

The Coastview Language Institute has small language classes. There are three levels of language classes at the Coastview Institute: beginning, intermediate, and advanced. Each classroom is furnished with fifteen comfortable chairs. Each room has a television and video equipment, shelves with books and games, and several cassette recorders. The walls of the classrooms are colorfully decorated with maps and posters. Each classroom has several large windows, which provide natural lighting. The classroom atmosphere at the Coastview Institute is cheerful, pleasant, and relaxing.

Now read over your underlined words quickly. Do they give the main ideas from the paragraph?

(*)

M. FACT OR OPINION

EXPLANATION: A **fact** is something that people generally agree is real or true. An **opinion** is an individual idea about something. Let us look at an example.

Imagine that it is a hot day, when the temperature is 35° Celsius (95° Fahrenheit). We can say,

Today is a very hot day.   FACT

But suppose one person says on this day,

This weather is great today!   OPINION

and another person says,

Today the weather is terrible.   OPINION

These two people have different opinions about hot weather: The first person likes it; the second person doesn't like it. The hot weather, however, is a fact.

Sometimes it is not so easy to distinguish facts from opinions. Therefore, your class might have some disagreements about the FACT OR OPINION exercises in this book. Discuss your differences in class. Do not worry if you cannot agree on every answer.

■ **Directions:**   Read the statements. Circle F is you believe that the statement is a fact. Circle O if you believe the statement is an opinion. (**Note:** See the exercise on AGREE/DISAGREE for examples of opinions.)

	Fact	Opinion
1. Classrooms from country to country are different in some ways.	F	O
2. Fluorescent light is white.	F	O
3. Fluorescent light is good in classrooms.	F	O
4. Good lighting is important in a classroom.	F	O
5. Maps are useful in a geography class.	F	O
6. More computers are in classrooms today than fifteen years ago.	F	O
7. Computers can teach languages very well.	F	O
8. Natural light is better than fluorescent or electric light.	F	O

What are some words that helped you figure out if the statement was a fact or an opinion?

⊛
N. PREDICT

■ **Directions:** Read the sentences. Imagine that they are the first sentences of complete paragraphs. What is the rest of the paragraph going to discuss? Make a guess (a prediction) by choosing one of the three possibilities. **Note:** One choice will be more *logical* than the others.

EXAMPLE: Some names can be both first and last names.

This paragraph is probably going to ___*c*___.
a. discuss first names
b. discuss last names
c. give examples of names that can be used as both first and last names

EXPLANATION: The phrase " . . . both first and last names" tells us that the paragraph will have something to do with these two kinds of names. Furthermore, it is logical to expect some examples of "Some names. . . . "

Teacher: You may want to explain topic sentences at this point. This decision will depend on the level or focus of your class.

---

1. In some ways classrooms around the world are similar.

   This paragraph is probably going to _____.
   a. discuss the similarities and differences among classrooms
   b. discuss the similarities among classrooms
   c. discuss the differences among classrooms

2. There are five units in this book.

   This paragraph is probably going to _____.
   a. name the five units
   b. discuss the Table of Contents and the Index of the book
   c. discuss two or three of the units in detail

3. A can is a metal container.

   This paragraph is probably going to _____.
   a. discuss cans, bottles, and jars
   b. give more details about cans
   c. discuss different kinds of metals

4. We can change the atmosphere of a room in several ways, but perhaps the easiest way is by changing the lighting.

   This paragraph is probably going to _____.
   a. discuss one way to change the atmosphere of a room

b. discuss several ways to change the atmosphere of a room

c. name all the ways to change the atmosphere of a room

5. A pleasant atmosphere in a classroom is important.

This paragraph is probably going to _____.

a. describe different kinds of classroom atmospheres

b. name several ways to change the atmosphere of a classroom

c. discuss why a pleasant classroom atmosphere is important

O. ACTIVITY: Discuss

■ Directions: Discuss the following questions in class:

1. What are high school classrooms like in your country?* (Discuss this question in relation to each section of the article, if you like.)

2. In your opinion, what is a good arrangement of chairs for a language class? Why?

EXTRA READING

Start Time _____

THE "BEST" STUDY ATMOSPHERE

1   Every student needs a place to study. Some students like to study in the
2   quiet atmosphere of a library. Most school libraries have large study tables with
3   many chairs. They also have individual study booths called *carrels*. A carrel is a
4   small table with "walls" or partitions around three sides. A carrel is for one
5   person, so there is only one chair at each carrel. Other students prefer to study
6   in their own rooms at home or in a dormitory. In their rooms, these students
7   have a desk, some bookshelves, and perhaps a study lamp to provide good light-
8   ing. All students need comfortable chairs because they spend many hours sitting.
9   Students have different ideas about the best atmosphere for studying. Some
10 students prefer one kind of lighting, one kind of table or desk, and one kind of
11 chair. Other students prefer a different kind of lighting and furniture. Some stu-
12 dents listen to music or study in groups. Other students need to be alone in a
13 quiet room. In other words, there is not one best atmosphere for studying: There
14 is a "best" atmosphere for each individual student.

TOTAL WORDS: 187   **End Time** _____

---

*"What is (or are) . . . like?" asks for *a description*.

Cartoon by Jim Nunn

Reflection

Think or talk about these questions:

Do you agree with the last sentence in this short article? Where do you study best? Why? Look at the cartoon. Do you know anyone who studies in this kind of atmosphere?

EXTRA READING 2

MEMORANDUM

To: Mr. Campbell and Staff
From: Dean Whitaker
Re: Preparation of Classrooms for Language Day
Date: October 19

As you know, next Saturday is Coastview Institute's Language Day. We need to prepare all the language classrooms for visitors and demonstrations. Before Friday evening, please check these classrooms: German (room 210), French (room 208), Spanish (room 211), Russian (room 215), Chinese (room 217), Japanese (room 219), and English as a Second Language (room 212). Here is what you need to do:

1. Arrange the classroom chairs in a semicircle. Put them against the wall, not in the middle of the room.

2. Put a small lectern on top of each teacher's desk.

3. Clean all blackboards.

4. Make sure that each room has maps and posters on the walls. (Mrs. Hall in the language laboratory has extras.)

5. Empty wastebaskets.

6. Put a cassette recorder and an overhead projector in each room.

Thank you very much for your help. We appreciate the work that you and your staff do. I'm sure Language Day will be a success.

Answer these questions:

1. What do you think a memorandum is?
2. Who wrote the memo?*
3. Who do you think Mr. Campbell is? What is his job?
4. What is going to happen next Saturday? (Describe activities that you think might happen.)
5. What do you think about the idea of a Language Day?

Memo is short for *memorandum*.

Chapter 4
Containers

Jamal El-Ayoubi

PREREADING

Ⓟ **Activity:** Identifying and Describing Containers

Materials: Containers of various kinds (bottles, jars, cans, tubes, boxes, bags, buckets); an assortment of tops (lids, caps, box tops); paper and pencil.

■ **Directions:**

> **Teacher:** Put the chart that follows on the board or on an overhead and go through one complete example (3a–e) with the whole class. In their groups, students should use each other (and you) as vocabulary resources, then dictionaries if necessary.

1. Divide the class into groups. Each group gets several different containers and their tops (if any).

2. One person in each group needs to make a chart like the example that follows. This person will write the group's answers.

Example Chart

Container	Material	Shape	Open and Close?	Function
1. bottle	*glass*	*tall, narrow*	*with a cap (screw-on)*	*to hold liquid*

3. Discuss questions a through e in your group. Write your answers on your chart.
- a. What is the name of each container?
- b. What material is each container made of?
- c. What is the shape of each container? (Tall or short? Wide or narrow? Deep or shallow? Round, cylindrical, square, rectangular . . . ?)
- d. Do the containers open and close? How do they open and close?
- e. What is the function of each container? (What is it used for?)

4. When you are finished, report the information on your chart to the whole class.

5. After the reports, put all the containers in the front of the class. Discuss some of these questions:
- a. Which containers usually contain liquids? Solids? Semisolids? Food (anything you can eat or drink)? Nonfoods? Chemicals? Can you think of anything else?
- b. Which containers do you find in the market? At home? At work (associated with a job or profession)?
- c. Are containers the same in all countries? What are some differences?

Teacher: Try to elicit at least one example of a different kind of container from each nationality represented in your class.

Survey

■ **Directions:** Look at the article "CONTAINERS." Follow the directions from your teacher. Answer on paper or orally.

1. What is the title of the article?

2. Look at the illustrations (figures). What is the title of each figure? Copy these on your paper (or give them orally).

3. Does the article have headings? What are they?

4. Does this article have a summary? Where? **Note:** A summary is important because it gives the most important information in just a few sentences.

Scan

■ **Directions:** Look at the article. Answer the following questions in writing or orally. All the questions ask about **materials** (metal, glass, plastic, and so on). The answers are in the first or second sentence of each section.

1. Find the section **Cans.** What are cans made of?

2. Find the section **Boxes and Cartons.** What are cartons made of?

3. Find the section **Jars.** What are jars made of?

4. Find the section **Bottles.** What are bottles made of?

5. Find the section **Bags.** What are many bags made of?

Listen

■ **Directions:** Your teacher will read all or part of the article "CONTAINERS" out loud. Follow silently in your book.

Underline

■ **Directions:** Go back to the beginning of the article. Your teacher will read silently with you and speak out loud the key words. Underline the key words as you hear them.

Skim

■ **Directions:** Now skim the entire article. (1) Read paragraph 2. It tells you something about the article. (2) Read all the headings; (3) read all your underlined key words; (4) look at the illustrations and their titles; and (5) read the Summary quickly.

Predict

■ **Directions:** Circle all the words that you think are important in this article. The first one is done for you.

(jars)	glass	lids	cans	flower
students	cookies	market	luggage	plastic
boxes	common	bottles	bags	chemist

Key Words

1 containers in . . . homes, schools,
     . . . places of work
2 this short article
   basic containers
3 can . . . metal container
     cylindrical
     open in different ways
4 "can of worms"
5 boxes and cartons . . . similar
     cardboard
     paper, wood, metal, or plastic
     rectangular or square
6 "to be boxed in"
7 jar . . . glass or ceramic container
     wide mouth
     no neck
     lids
     practical
8 " . . . hand in the cookie jar"

9 bottle
     glass
     plastic
     small mouth . . . neck
     caps
10 bottle brush
11 bottleneck
12 bag . . . flexible container
     paper, foil, . . . plastic
     folding
     sealing
13 brown paper bags
     American markets
     to bag
     "bagger"
14 many hundreds of containers
     everyday life
     profession
15 Summary

SILENT READING

■ **Directions:** Now read the entire article. Try to read carefully, but quickly. Be prepared to describe several of the containers briefly.

CONTAINERS

1   We can find containers in our homes, schools, and places of work. For example, food and nonfood products are sold in containers. A favorite container of students and teachers is the wastebasket. Of course, containers are an important part of many professions: Painters, doctors, biologists, photographers, chemists, and others use many kinds of specialized containers.

2   In this short article, it is not possible to discuss all kinds of containers. Therefore, let us look at some of the simple and basic containers. We will name them, identify their shapes and the materials they are made of, and say a few words about lids and tops. We will also look at some expressions in English that use images of containers.

Cans

3   A can is a metal container. It is usually cylindrical[1] in shape, and may have a paper label on the outside. The name of the product is printed on the label or on the metal itself (Figure 1). Cans open in different ways, depending on the product. We need a can opener to open some cans; this utensil cuts the metal. Paint cans have lids that we must pry up with a special tool. Beverage cans have a pop top or a ring top. Spray cans have a push-button top. Cans are durable containers.

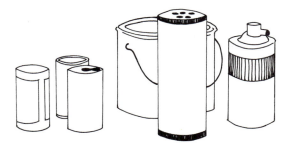

Figure 1.   Cans.

4   English has a very graphic, informal expression to describe a difficult and complicated situation. We call such a situation a "can of worms." If we knowingly get into a difficult and complicated situation, we "open a can of worms."

Boxes and Cartons

5   Boxes and cartons are similar containers. Cartons are usually made of cardboard (heavy paper), and as a result are not very durable. Boxes can be made of cardboard, paper, wood, metal, or plastic. Boxes and cartons have rectangular or square sides (Figure 2). Some of these containers, such as jewelry boxes and egg

Figure 2.   Boxes and cartons.

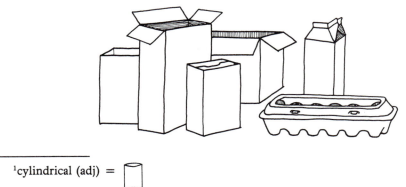

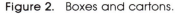

[1]cylindrical (adj) =

cartons, have tops that open and close with hinges. Other boxes and cartons have removable tops or tops that fold together. (**Note:** It is not always clear why we use the word *box* in one case and the word *carton* in another case.)

6   An expression that uses the image of a box is "to be boxed in." We imagine a person who is surrounded by four walls and cannot escape. A person in a very small, closed office is boxed in, and so is a person who cannot escape from his thoughts.

Jars

7   A jar is a glass or ceramic container. It has a wide mouth (top opening) and no neck. Some jars have screw-on lids (also called *tops* or *covers*), and other jars have lids that fit inside the mouth (Figure 3). Some jars (e.g.,[2] jars you see in supermarkets) are very practical[3] because they hold many different products, and because we can clean them and use them again. Jars are durable but breakable.

Figure 3. Jars.

8   A popular expression uses the image of a jar: "I caught you with your hand in the cookie jar." We imagine a small child stealing cookies. But the expression is also used with adults who get caught as they try secretly to do something wrong, such as stealing money from their own company.

Bottles

9   A bottle, like a jar, is a container that is usually made of glass. These days, however, plastic bottles are also very common (Figure 4). Bottles are different from jars in one important way: A bottle has a small mouth and a neck, but a jar has a wide mouth and no neck.[4] Most bottles have caps or tops that either screw on or snap on. Bottles hold beverages (juice, soda, etc.[5]) and other liquid

---

[2]e.g. (Latin, *exempli gratia*) = for example

[3]practical (adj) = useful

[4]One exception to this definition is the *pill bottle* (e.g., bottles for vitamins, aspirin, medicine tablets). Another exception is the *ink bottle*. We call these containers "bottles," but they look like small jars.

[5]etc. (Latin) = *et cetera* ("and so on"); more examples are possible

Figure 4.   Bottles.

food. They are also used to contain photographic, industrial, and medical chemicals.

10   A plant that has a colorful red flower is called a *bottle brush plant.* A real bottle brush (i.e.,[6] a brush that is used to clean bottles) and the bottle brush flower look very similar (Figure 5).

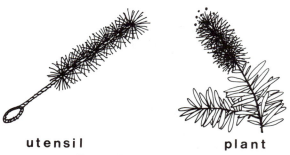

utensil   **plant**

Figure 5.   Bottle brushes.

11   Another word that uses the image of a bottle is *bottleneck.* A bottleneck is a special kind of traffic jam.[7] It happens on large highways where several lanes come together into fewer lanes. If many cars merge from three lanes into one lane, for example, they will create a bottleneck and traffic will slow down (Figure 6).

Bags

12   A bag is a flexible[8] container. Many bags are made of paper, foil, or thin plastic. Such bags are not durable containers—we usually throw them away. We

---

[6]i.e. (Latin, *id est*) = that is to say; in other words; to explain further

[7]a (traffic) jam (n, C) = a difficult, problematic situation, e.g., when cars cannot move on the highway

[8]flexible (adj) = soft and movable

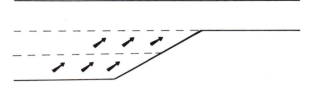

Figure 6.   A bottleneck.

close bags in several ways, for example by folding them, by tying them with something, and, in the case of plastic bags, by knotting them or sealing[9] them with heat (Figure 7). Bags come in many sizes and contain many different products. We also use the word *bag* to describe more durable containers, such as purses and luggage.

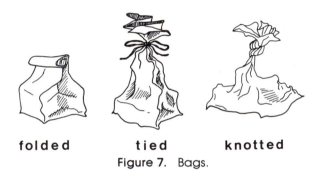

folded   **tied**   **knotted**
Figure 7.   Bags.

13   When Americans hear the word *bag,* they probably think first of the brown paper bags at the checkstands in American markets. Markets use *millions* of brown paper bags every year for customers' groceries. The customers save the bags and use them again for other purposes. The verb *to bag* means to put things (e.g., groceries) into a bag. A "bagger" is a person who works in a market putting groceries in bags for customers. In some other countries, people must bring their own bags to the market. String bags are popular for this purpose.

CONCLUSION

14   The containers mentioned in this article are just a few of many hundreds of different containers. We have not talked about tubes, tubs, bins, baskets, vats, vases, casks, drums, flasks, trays, or tanks. We have not mentioned containers that we use in cooking and serving food. We have not talked about containers by profession: Painters use cans for paint; photographers use bottles and trays for chemicals; chemists use beakers and test tubes. What containers do you have

---

[9]to seal (v) = to close very securely (well, tightly) so that nothing can get out

around you in your everyday life? What containers do you use in your profession? Can you imagine a world without containers?

SUMMARY

15   This article describes five common containers: (1) cans, (2) boxes and cartons, (3) jars, (4) bottles, and (5) bags. These containers are made of materials such as metal, glass, paper, and plastic. Some of these containers have tops that screw on, snap on, or fit on. We must open other containers with special tools. We can fold, tie, or seal containers such as bags. We can find the names of containers in other expressions in English. There are hundreds of specialized containers.

EXERCISES _____

⊛
A. COMPREHENSION CHECK: Recall

▪ **Directions:**   Give a brief description of several of the containers in the article.

_____

Teacher: If you do this recall task in small groups, you might see which group can recall the most (and the most accurate) information.

_____

⊛
B. COMPREHENSION CHECK: Fill in the Blank

▪ **Directions:**   Fill in the blank with an appropriate word. There might be more than one good answer.

EXAMPLE: Painters, photographers, and ___*chemists*___ use containers in their work.

1. Jars, bottles, bags, and boxes are all examples of _____.

2. Two kinds of containers that are often made of glass are _____ and _____.

3. Cans are usually made of _____.

4. Boxes are made of different materials such as _____ and _____.

5. Jars have a wide _____ and bottles have a small

_____.

6. We can find containers _____, at school, and at work.

C. COMPREHENSION CHECK: Multiple Choice

■ **Directions:**　Choose the best answer. Write the letter in the blank.

1. This article discusses _____.
   a. containers in supermarkets
   b. five basic containers
   c. containers used by chemists and photographers
   d. glass containers

2. Bottles are usually made of _____.
   a. paper or plastic
   b. glass or cardboard
   c. metal or wood
   d. glass or plastic

3. Boxes, jars, and bottles open and close with different _____.
   a. materials
   b. containers
   c. tops
   d. expressions

4. One important difference between a jar and a bottle is _____.
   a. the material it is made of
   b. the size of the mouth
   c. the label
   d. the size of the container

5. A *bottleneck* on the highway is _____.
   a. part of a bottle
   b. a plant
   c. a cleaning utensil
   d. a traffic problem

6. This article does *not* discuss _____.
   a. containers used in different professions
   b. bags, bottles, jars, and boxes
   c. expressions that use the names of containers
   d. materials that containers are made of

D. SELECTIVE READING: Categorize, Cross out

■ **Directions:**   Underline the general category word in each line. Cross out the word that does not belong. Work quickly.

EXAMPLE: Bob   <u>first name</u>   Joyce   ~~Mr.~~   Charles   Alice

1. bag   size   jar   box   container   bottle   carton

2. desk   furniture   chair   bed   chalk   table   lectern

3. metal   bag   plastic   paper   foil   material   glass

4. liquids   Coca-Cola   water   bottle   juice   tea

5. Johnson   Sanchez   last name   Wilson   Smith   John

6. two   first   third   fourth   ninth   ordinal number

7. parts of a textbook   chapters   language textbooks   headings   table of contents   index   units

E. SELECTIVE READING: Identify and Underline

■ **Directions:**   Read the sentences. Underline all the words that name containers and materials. (Do not underline the words *container* and *material*.) Work quickly.

Teacher: These sentences are purposely difficult. Students should practice tolerating partial comprehension.

EXAMPLE: A <u>wastebasket</u> is a household or office container that is often made of <u>plastic</u>.

1. Wastebaskets that are made of straw or cardboard are not nearly as durable as those that are made of metal or heavy plastic.

2. Many years ago, most milk was sold in glass bottles. Today milk usually comes in cartons or plastic bottles.

3. A garbage can is a large outdoor container made of metal or durable plastic. Garbage cans ordinarily have tight-fitting lids with handles.

4. Some containers, such as bins, dumpsters, and barrels, are quite large and used primarily outdoors or in warehouses and factories. These containers must be sturdy and long-lasting. For this reason they are made of heavy metal or strong wood.

5. Some containers, such as vases, serve a decorative purpose. Vases come in a variety of materials, but some of the most beautiful vases are made of glass and porcelain.

(*)

F. WORD ASSOCIATION

EXPLANATION: When you hear or see the word *English,* what do you think of? Here are some possibilities: *language, studying, classes, teachers, students, difficult* (or *easy*), *grammar.* Each person will think of different words. Write *your* words on the line:

English: _____

_____

■ Directions: Look at each word. What do you think of when you see each word? Write all the words you can think of on the line. Discuss the words in class. (Remember: There are no correct answers. *All* the answers are good.)

1. plastic _____

_____

2. books _____

_____

3. liquids _____

_____

4. bag _____

_____

5. bottle _____

_____

G. PARAPHRASE

■ Directions: Read the pairs of sentences. Circle S if the meaning of the two sentences is the same or similar. Circle D if the meaning of the two sentences is different.

	Same	**Different**
1. a. A can is a metal container. b. A can is a container made of metal.	S	D
2. a. Both food products and nonfood products come in containers. b. We can find food products and nonfood products in the supermarket.	S	D

	Same	Different
3. a. A "bagger" is a person who puts groceries in bags at the supermarket. b. People who work in supermarkets putting groceries in bags are called "baggers."	S	D
4. a. Glass, metal, and paper are examples of materials. b. Some containers are made of glass, metal, and paper.	S	D
5. a. Jars and bottles are similar in some ways. b. Jars and bottles are different in some ways.	S	D

H. LEVELS OF GENERALIZATION

■ **Directions:** Look at the groups of three words. In each group, one word is **general,** one word is **specific,** and one word is **more specific.** Write G after the general word. Write S after the specific word. Write MS after the more specific word.

        EXAMPLE: first name ___S___

                name ___G___

                John ___MS___

1. small table _____

   furniture _____

   table _____

2. language students _____

   English language students _____

   students _____

3. rooms _____

   small classrooms _____

   classrooms _____

4. ballpoint pens _____

   pens _____

   writing utensils _____

5. books _____

   language textbooks _____

   textbooks _____

6. Asian country _____

   country _____

   Japan _____

7. number _____

   2nd (second) _____

   ordinal number _____

8. Bob _____

   name _____

   nickname _____

⊛

I. ANALOGIES

■ **Directions:** Read each pair of words. Each pair shows a relationship between the two words. Then look at the word in boldface. Circle the word from the line of words that shows the same relationship. Then write that word in the blank. Work quickly.

EXAMPLE 1: book:read **pen:** _write_

pencil   read   write   paper

EXPLANATION: The word *write* completes the analogy: We read books; we write with pens. We can read the analogy this way: "Book is to read as pen is to write."

EXAMPLE 2: knife:fork **pen:** _pencil_

pencil   read   write   paper

EXPLANATION: This time, we need to choose another noun in order to form a set, or an expected pair (words that we often hear together in pairs). The words knife and fork go together, and the words pen and pencil do, too. "Knife is to fork as pen is to pencil."

1. can:container   **chair:**_____

table   furniture   desk   wood

2. jar:glass   **can:**_____

metal   container   worms   cylinder

3. square:shape   **red:**_____

size   length   pretty   color

4. Susan:first name   **Johnson:**_____

first name   middle name   last name

middle initial

5. "bagger":market   **secretary:**_____

woman   office   desk   type

6. water:liquid   **apple:**_____

fruit   red   good   solid

7. prayer book:church   **textbook:**_____

                                  student   read   school   study

8. word:sentence   **paragraph:**_____

                                  article   words   footnote   part

J. LOGICAL WORD GROUPS

■ **Directions:**   Read the paragraph from the article "CONTAINERS" in (a) vertical logical word groups, (b) horizontal logical word groups, and (c) with normal spacing.

a. Vertical

A bottle,
like a jar,
is a container
that is usually made of glass.
These days,
however,
plastic bottles
are also very common.
Bottles
are different from jars
in one important way:
A bottle
has a small mouth and a neck,
but a jar
has a wide mouth and no neck.
Most bottles
have caps or tops
that either screw on
or snap on.

b. Horizontal

A bottle,   like a jar,   is a container   that is usually made of glass.   These days,   however,   plastic bottles   are also very common.   Bottles   are different from jars   in one important way: A bottle   has a small mouth and a neck,   but a jar   has a wide mouth and no neck.   Most bottles   have caps or tops   that either screw on   or snap on.

c. Normal Spacing

A bottle, like a jar, is a container that is usually made of glass. These days, however, plastic bottles are also very common. Bottles are different from jars in one important way: A bottle has a small mouth and a neck, but a jar has a wide mouth and no neck. Most bottles have caps or tops that either screw on or snap on.

K. REFERENCE: *this, these*

■ **Directions:** Read the sentences. The underlined pronouns and noun phrases refer to a noun phrase in the first sentence. Write the noun phrase from the first sentence in the blank.

> **Teacher:** In this exercise students need to find the referent for noun phrases such as *this metal* and *these containers* as well as for pronouns. Have students ask themselves: Which metal? Which containers?

1. A can is a metal container. <u>It</u> is usually cylindrical in shape.

It = _____

2. Lids fit on the tops of containers. <u>They</u> screw on or snap on.

They = _____

3. Many beverage cans are made of aluminum. <u>This metal</u> is lightweight.

This metal = _____

4. Cartons and boxes are often made of heavy paper. <u>These containers</u> are typically square or rectangular.

These containers = _____

5. Textbooks have tables of contents and indexes. <u>These sections</u> can help you find information quickly and easily.

These sections = _____

6. Americans like first names and nicknames. However, <u>they</u> don't use <u>these names</u> all the time.

they = _____

these names = _____

L. GUESS

■ **Directions:** Choose the best general meaning of the underlined word. Use the other words in the sentences to help you guess.

1. <u>Bare</u> walls can create a clean and simple atmosphere in a room. However, many people prefer walls of different colors and patterns.

Bare walls are probably _____.
a. walls with windows
b. walls without anything on them
c. walls with pictures and maps

2. The walls of many language classrooms are covered with pictures, maps, and <u>posters</u>.

Posters are _____.
a. a kind of picture
b. a kind of machine
c. things to write with

3. Some classrooms for children have a <u>pleasant and cheerful</u> atmosphere. These rooms are colorful and decorated with pictures of animals and plants. Interesting toys and games are on shelves around the room.

Pleasant and cheerful means _____.
a. large and open
b. quiet and serious
c. nice and happy

4. Cardboard boxes and paper bags are similar in two ways: They are both containers and they are both paper products. However, the paper of paper bags is thin and flexible; cardboard is thick and <u>stiff</u>.

Stiff means _____.
a. printed with colors
b. not flexible
c. thin

5. Most supermarkets sell empty plastic containers with lids for storing food. Some people prefer <u>Tupperware</u>, because it is good quality and has very tight-fitting lids. It is not possible to buy <u>Tupperware</u> at a store, however.

Tupperware is _____.
a. a special kind of tight-fitting lid
b. the name of a store
c. the name of special plastic containers

6. Some containers, such as cans, are very <u>durable</u>. They are not damaged or broken easily. Other containers, such as bags and boxes, are not so strong and long-lasting.

Durable means _____.
a. breakable
b. strong
c. sealed

(*)
M. ACTIVITY: Vocabulary Survey

■ Directions: Sometimes people have different words for the same containers. In this activity, you need to ask people outside of class to give you the names for the containers shown on the chart that follows. When you return to class, compare all the vocabulary items on each chart. Do people agree on the names of the containers? What differences did you find?

Teacher: Each student can interview one person, preferably a native English speaker. Prepare them for this activity by practicing *introductions, explanation of task* ("I'm doing a vocabulary survey"), *requests* ("Can you help me?" "How do you spell that?"), and *closings* ("Thank you for your help").

Containers

Diagram	Name

Diagram	Name

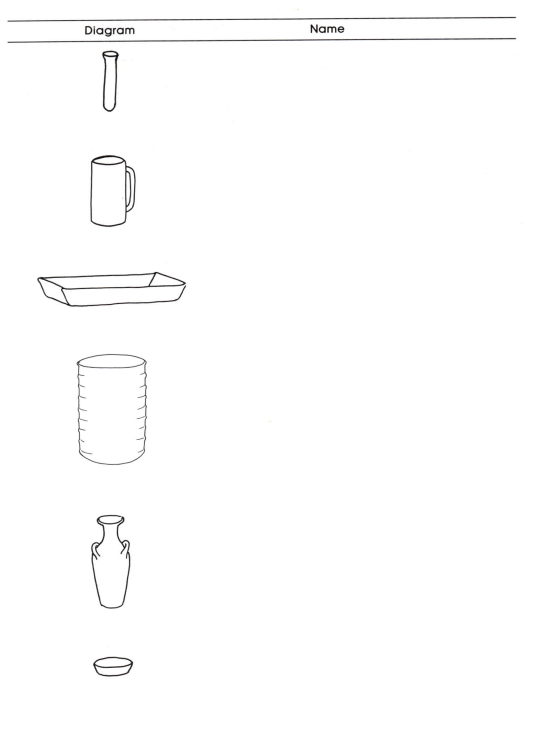

EXTRA READING

Start Time _____

SUPERMARKET CONTAINERS

1   Are you familiar with large supermarkets? If so, then you probably know
2   that almost everything in the market is in a container. Most food is in containers.
3   Even fresh meat is sold in plastic packages. Fresh fruit and vegetables are usually
4   the only food items that do not come in containers. In fact, almost everything
5   at the supermarket is in a bag, a box, a bottle, a jar, a carton, or a can.
6   This kind of packaging system is necessary at large supermarkets. Super-
7   markets buy large quantities of everything. Products must be protected during
8   shipment and they must sit on shelves for long periods of time. Containers, there-
9   fore, protect the products. Containers have another function, too. They give in-
10 formation about each product—names, weights, materials, and ingredients, and
11 sometimes pictures of the products. This information is printed on labels or on
12 the containers directly.
13   But think of this: *We never see* most of the things we buy at the supermarket
14 until we get home and open the containers. When we go shopping, we look at
15 the *labels* on the containers. If the container is made of glass or clear plastic,
16 perhaps we can see a little bit of the product. But usually containers completely
17 hide their products. Shoppers must trust the labels.

TOTAL WORDS: 212   **End Time** _____

Reflection

Think or talk about these questions:

In your country, what products usually come in containers? What products do
not? In your opinion, what are the advantages and disadvantages of containers?
What information is on a label?

EXTRA READING 2

drum \drəm\ *n*   **1.** a percussion instrument that consists of a hollow cylinder
with a material such as animal skin stretched over one or both ends; the
skin is beaten with sticks or with the hands to produce a sound   **2.** the
sound of a drum   **3.** something, such as part of a machine, that has
the shape of a drum   **4.** a large container in the shape of a drum; such
a container is usually made of metal and holds liquids; capacity is between
50 and 450 liters (12 to 110 gallons)

Answer the questions:

1. Where is this selection from? What do we call this kind of selection?
2. What part of speech is the word *drum* here (noun or verb)?
3. Can you draw a drum from this definition? Try it.
4. Which definition describes a drum as part of a machine? As a sound? As a musical instrument? As a container?
5. Which definition of a drum fits this chapter in your book?
6. What kinds of liquids do you think might go in a drum?

Chapter 5
Supplies: A Personal Essay

Jamal El-Ayoubi

PREREADING

Ⓟ **Activity:** Matching People and Supplies

Materials: Two or three groups of basic supplies (tools, equipment), including the seven in this article. They should be grouped around a profession: hammer, nails, screwdriver; paint brushes, paint, other artist's materials, and so on.

- Directions:

Teacher: Put all the supplies in random arrangement in a place where all students can see them. It is not necessary to name each object; students need only to recognize what they are. If possible, let students work together. Provide them with vocabulary when necessary.

---

1. Look at all the objects. They are supplies (perhaps also tools and equipment) that different people use. Ask yourself: What kinds of people use these supplies? What are the jobs or interests of these people?

2. Now arrange all the objects into groups according to who uses the objects. There is probably more than one logical arrangement. Examples are: teacher's supplies, student's supplies, carpenter's tools, and artist's supplies.

3. Now write the objects by group on the blackboard. Your teacher will help you with vocabulary and spelling.

	Teacher	**Student**	**Carpenter**
EXAMPLE:	paper	notebook	hammer
	pens	pens and pencils	nails
	paper clips	eraser	screwdriver
	stapler	. . .	. . .
	. . .		

Survey

■ Directions: Look at the article. Follow these directions from your teacher.

1. What is the title of this article? Is there a subtitle (another title under the main title)? Write the title and the subtitle on your paper.

2. Are there any headings in this article?

3. Are there any illustrations? If so, what are they?

4. Are there any titles or labels with the illustrations?

Scan

■ Directions: Look at the article. Choose three consecutive paragraphs (e.g., 2, 3, and 4). How many times does the writer use the pronoun *I* in these paragraphs?

Key Words

1   Some things are necessary
     little things
     we use every day

2   a writer and a teacher
     my basic supplies

3   first
     pencil sharpener
       sharp pencils
       want to work

4   second
     scissors
       four pairs
       different purpose

5   third
     scotch tape
       two holders

6 fourth
   stapler
      good quality
      large
7 fifth
   paper clips
      use a hundred
      lose a hundred
8 sixth
   paper
      too much paper

9 seventh
   string
      a hundred . . . uses
      keep all . . . string
      drawer . . . full of string
10 every person's list is different
   tells us something about a person

Listen

▪ **Directions:** Listen while your teacher reads part of the article "SUPPLIES: A PERSONAL ESSAY" out loud. Follow silently in your book.

Underline

▪ **Directions:** Go to the beginning of the article. Your teacher will read silently and speak out loud only the key words. Follow in your book and underline the key words as you hear them.

Skim

▪ **Directions:** Prepare simple reading notes as you skim by writing the information from items 1 and 2.

1. Read the first sentence of paragraph 3. It says: "The first, and probably most important, item on my list of necessary supplies is a pencil sharpener." On your paper, write *1st* (*first* in number form). Then write the noun *pencil sharpener* after the number:

1st   pencil sharpener

2. Continue skimming and taking notes from paragraphs 4, 5, 6, 7, 8, and 9. Write a number (2nd, 3rd . . .) and a noun that names a supply for each paragraph. Write in list form.

3. Continue skimming. Look at the illustrations again; read your underlined words; read the last paragraph (10).

Predict

■ **Directions:**   Read the statements. Circle A if you agree. Circle D if you disagree.

1. The writer of this article probably works in a restaurant.   A   D
2. The supplies that the writer talks about are also useful for students.   A   D
3. This article probably has some humor in it (parts that make you smile).   A   D

SILENT READING

■ **Directions:**   Now read the entire article silently and carefully. Read as quickly as you can. Be prepared to compare the author's basic supply list with your own supply list.

SUPPLIES:
A Personal Essay

1   Some things are necessary in life. I'm not talking about the big things, like food, water, shelter, and love. I'm talking about the little things, the small necessities that we have in our homes, schools, and offices. I'm talking about the items that we use every day without thinking.

2   We can make a list of a hundred different kinds of supplies if we want to, but I'm going to talk about just a few of them. I'm a writer and a teacher, so for the most part my basic supplies are things that I need for writing and teaching. People have different basic supplies, depending on their interests and their professions. Here are mine. While you're reading this, think about the little things that are essential in your life.

3   The first, and probably most important, item on my list of necessary supplies is a pencil sharpener. I can't work without sharp pencils. Of course, everybody is different—I'm speaking only for myself. When I see sharp pencils on my desk, I want to work. But when I see dull pencils, I forget about my work and think only about sharpening the pencils. I have several pencil sharpeners in my house and in my office. Here is a sketch of a couple of them:

4   The second item on my list of basic supplies is a pair of scissors. I like scissors, and I use them to cut many different things. In fact, I have four pairs

of scissors, and I use each pair for a different purpose. In this sketch, you can see several different kinds of scissors:

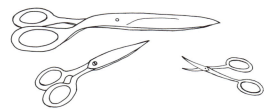

5   The third item on my list is scotch tape. I tape papers to papers, papers to walls and doors, papers to our refrigerator, and papers to the mirror. You can see from the sketch that I have two kinds of scotch tape holders: a big holder and a small holder. The small scotch tape holders are useful sometimes, but I don't like them. They're flimsy and breakable, and you need two hands to use them. I can use my big holder with one hand, because it's very heavy and solid.

6   A stapler is the fourth item on my list. I have a good stapler. It's solid—very good quality—and quite large. It holds a lot of staples. It can staple twenty or thirty pieces of paper together. Here is a drawing of my stapler:

7   The fifth item on my list of necessities is paper clips. Here is a little sketch of a paper clip:

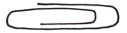

I probably use a hundred of these little things every week. ·I probably lose a hundred of them a week, too. That's the problem with paper clips—they're very small. I drop them everywhere. Then I find them later on the floor, in my pockets, in my typewriter, in the washing machine, in the rug, and even in my coffee cup now and then. The cat likes to play with them on the linoleum floor, so I always leave a couple of them there.

8   Sixth on my list of basic supplies is paper. My house and office are full of paper—clean paper, used paper, large pieces of paper, small pieces of paper, notebook paper, scratch paper, drawing paper, graph paper, computer paper, school paper, letter-writing paper. I think that too much paper is a problem that both students and teachers have. Sometimes I feel buried in paper, as you can see from this cartoon:

9   Seventh and last on my list is string. String has a hundred different uses, but right now I can't think of any. I keep all pieces of string that are long enough to tie in a knot. I can't throw away string. We have a drawer in the kitchen that is full of string—long pieces of string, medium pieces of string, short pieces of string, balls of new string, balls of used string. Our cat loves to play in this drawer, needless to say. Here is a sketch of our cat, Chibi, in the string drawer:

10   Let me finish up by saying that these seven items on my basic supply list are seven out of perhaps two dozen. I use these supplies every day in my house or in my office. Every person can think of a basic supply list, and I'm sure that every person's list is different. Such a list tells us something about a person—job, interests, habits. Can you look at my list now and say something about me?

> pencil sharpener
> scissors
> scotch tape
> stapler
> paper clips
> paper
> string

EXERCISES

A. COMPREHENSION CHECK: True or False

■ **Directions:** Read the statements. Write T after the statements that are true in relation to the article. Write F after the statements that are false.

1. The writer of this article uses the first person (*I, me, my, we, our*).   _____

2. One of the items on the writer's basic supply list is paper clips.   _____

3. The writer lists a typewriter as a basic supply.   _____

4. The writer uses a lot of paper.   _____

5. The writer's dog plays with the paper clips and the string.   _____

B. COMPREHENSION CHECK: Multiple Choice

■ **Directions:** Read the statements and questions. Choose the answer that completes the statements or answers the questions. Write the letter in the blank.

1. This article is different from the other articles (Chapters 1 through 4) because it is written in the first person (*I, my, we* . . .). What is another way in which this article is different from the other articles? _____
   a. It does not discuss objects.
   b. It does not have any headings or subheadings.
   c. It does not have any organization.

2. One item is mentioned in several different sections of the article. That item is _____.
   a. paper
   b. scotch tape
   c. scissors

3. The writer of the article believes that _____.
   a. every person uses the same basic supplies
   b. teachers and writers have more supplies than other people
   c. we can learn something about people by knowing what supplies they use every day

4. We can describe this article as _____.
   a. formal and not personal
   b. informal and personal
   c. not organized

C. COMPREHENSION CHECK: Recall

■ **Directions:**   Try to remember all the items that the writer talked about. In what order did she talk about them? What did she say about them? Are some of the items in the article on *your* basic supply list?

D. SELECTIVE READING: Identify and Underline

■ **Directions:**   Read the sentences. Underline all the nouns that name supplies or tools. Do not worry if you do not understand all the sentences completely. Work as quickly as possible.

   EXAMPLE: The writer has a large collection of sharp <u>pencils</u>.

1. People usually store pens, pencils, paper clips, rulers, and scissors in the top drawer of their desks.
2. Several dozen paper clips are somewhere under the dining room table.
3. I keep a supply of typewriter paper and notebook paper in the house and in the office.
4. Dull knives are an irritation and a nuisance.
5. There is a drawer in the kitchen that is full of string, paper clips, and old pencils.
6. Scissors are useful items to have around the house, and so is scotch tape.
7. It is difficult to imagine a carpenter without certain basic tools such as a hammer, a screwdriver, and a drill.
8. Straight pins, safety pins, and thumbtacks are items that frequently end up on the floor.

E. SELECTIVE READING: Categorize, Cross Out

■ **Directions:** Read the line of words. In each line, there is one word that does not belong. Cross it out. Write the category to which the other words belong on the line. Work as quickly as possible.

EXAMPLE: large   small   old   nice   ~~chair~~   interesting

adjectives

1. cup   table   plate   bowl   glass   mug

_____

2. paper   pencils   pens   paper clips   cats   staplers

_____

3. knife   sharp   old   dull   big   heavy

_____

4. classroom   teacher   office   kitchen   bedroom   bathroom

_____

5. television   cassette   video   shelf   computer   radio

_____

6. empty   box   familiar   new   useful   full

_____

⊛

F. SELECTIVE READING: Identify Synonyms

■ **Directions:** Look at the word in parentheses. Then read the sentence. In the sentence, there is a **synonym** of the word in parentheses. A synonym is a word that has a similar meaning to another word. Underline the synonym in the sentence.

EXAMPLE: (large) Most language classrooms are not very <u>big.</u>

1. (nice) A pleasant atmosphere in a classroom helps people study.
2. (not noisy) Libraries are usually quiet, relaxing places to study.
3. (not sharp) Some people do not enjoy writing with old, dull pencils.
4. (strong and long-lasting) Some of the best and most durable tools are very old.
5. (not stiff) One difference between paper and cardboard is that paper is thin and flexible, but cardboard is thick and stiff.
6. (basic) The main point of this exercise is to provide practice with synonyms.

⊛

G. SCAN

A. Contractions

■ Directions: Look at the following sentences. Each sentence has a **contraction** in it:

> I'm reading the directions.   (*I'm* = a contraction for *I am*.)
> We're studying English. (*We're* = a contraction for *we are*.)
> I don't understand.   (*don't* = a contraction for *do not*.)
> This exercise isn't difficult.   (*isn't* = a contraction for *is not*.)

We use contractions in speaking all the time. However, we do not use contractions in writing all the time. Formal written English does not use many contractions. Contractions are acceptable in informal written English.

Now look at the article from this chapter. It is written in an informal style. Circle all the contractions in the article. **Note:** Be careful—one word looks like a contraction, but it is not. It is a possessive: every perso*n's* list.

B. Countable (C) and Uncountable (U) Nouns

Teacher: The lists that students will make may differ. The directions do not ask students to find *all* the nouns in a paragraph.

■ Directions: The article in this chapter has many examples of countable and uncountable nouns (C and U nouns). Can you find them? Make a list on a piece of paper.
  a. Look at paragraph 1. Find four examples of singular U nouns. Find four examples of plural C nouns.
  b. Look at paragraph 4. Find one example of a plural U noun. Find two examples of plural C nouns.
  c. Look at paragraph 8. Find one example of a singular U noun. Find four examples of singular C nouns. Find three examples of plural C nouns.

⊛

H. REFERENCE: *one, another, the other . . .*

EXPLANATION: Sometimes sentences have some words left out (i.e., omitted), but we understand them anyway. Look at the following sentences:

  a. My family has two cars. <u>One</u> is a Datsun. <u>The other</u> is a Plymouth.

> Question: One *what?* ————→ Answer: One *car* (of the two cars).
> Question: The other *what?* ————→ Answer: The other *car* (of the two cars).

We can say that *one* (a pronoun) refers back to the noun phrase *two cars* in the first sentence. We can say that *the other* (also a pronoun) refers back to *two cars,* too.

Again: My family has <u>two cars</u>. <u>One</u> is a Datsun. <u>The other</u> is a Plymouth.

Now look at these sentences:

b. This book has two kinds of reading articles. <u>The first</u> is the long chapter article. <u>The second</u> is the short reading at the end of the chapter.

> Question: The first *what?* ⟶ Answer: The first *kind of reading article* (of the two kinds).
> Question: The second *what?* ⟶ Answer: The second *kind of reading article* (of the two kinds).

We can say that *the first* and *the second* refer back to the noun phrase *two kinds of reading articles.*

Again: This book has <u>two kinds of reading articles</u>. <u>The first</u> is the long chapter article. <u>The second</u> is the short reading at the end of the chapter.

Note: In both examples a and b, the words *one, the other, the first,* and *the second* are singular. They refer to one thing among two or more things. (Other pronouns, such as *some* and [*the*] *others,* can be used to refer to more than one thing.)

Teacher: If appropriate for your class, you might demonstrate how sentences such as these examples become repetitive if they are written out completely. **Note:** When used without their nouns, words such as *one, the other,* etc., are pronouns. With their nouns, they function as determiners.

Now look at the lists of words and the example sentences that follow. Each list is in sequential order (from first to last). The nouns in parentheses are not necessary, because we understand the sentences without them.

Teacher: You will note that some variation in these lists is possible.

Group of 2 | I need <u>two books</u> for this class.
one (book) | **One** is a reading book.
the other (book) | **The other** is a grammar book.

Group of 3 | I have <u>three roommates</u>.
one (roommate) | **One** is from Japan.
another (roommate) | **Another** is from Indonesia.
the other (roommate) | **The other** is from Switzerland.

Group of 4 or More	My family gave me <u>five presents</u>.
one (present)	**One** was a dictionary.
another (present)	**Another** was a sweater.
the next (present)	**The next** was a ballpoint pen.
another (present)	**Another** was writing paper and envelopes.
the last (present)	**The last** was stamps.

We may also use ordinal numbers as pronouns:

Group of 2 or More	I'm taking _____ classes.
the first (class)	**The first** is a math class.
the second (class)	**The second** is an English class.
the third (class)	**The third** is a history class.
the . . . th (class)	The **. . . th** is a . . . class.
the last (class)	**The last** is a . . . class.

■ **Directions:** Now read the groups of sentences. The underlined words refer back to a noun phrase in the first sentence. Ask yourself: One *what?* The other *what?* The second *what?* Write your answer in the blank. **Note:** In this exercise, the underlined words are all singular. They refer back to *one* thing from the group of things in the first sentence. Therefore, the word that you write in the blank needs to be singular.

> EXAMPLE: This exercise has two parts. <u>The first</u> is an explanation. <u>The second</u> is practice.
>
> The first _____*part*_____
> The second ____*part*_____

1. There are two tables in the classroom. <u>One</u> is small and <u>the other</u> is large.

    One _____

    the other _____

2. Most Americans have three names. <u>The first</u> is a given name, <u>the second</u> is a middle name, and <u>the third</u> is a family name.

    The first _____

    the second _____

    the third _____

3. I have three textbooks this term. <u>One</u> is a grammar book, <u>another</u> is a reader, and <u>the other</u> is a composition book.

One _____

another _____

the other _____

4. The four foreign students in my dormitory are all from different countries. <u>One</u> is from Japan, <u>another</u> is from Kuwait, <u>another</u> is from Mexico, and <u>the last</u> is from Switzerland.

One _____

another _____

another _____

the last _____

5. I use three basic supplies every day. <u>One</u> is a drawing pen. <u>Another</u> is artist's paper. <u>The other</u> is black ink.

One _____

Another _____

The other _____

6. Three kinds of containers are used to hold and protect liquids and semisolids. <u>The first</u>, and perhaps the most durable, is a can. <u>The next</u> is a jar. <u>The last</u> is a bottle.

The first _____

The next _____

The last _____

I. ORDER: Sequential

■ **Directions:** Read the sentences. They are not in the correct order. They are in random order. Put a number by each sentence to show a more logical order.

EXAMPLE: __*3*__ The other is a Plymouth.

__*1*__ My family has two cars.

__*2*__ One is a Datsun.

1. _____ Another is a stove.

_____ One is a refrigerator.

_____ The other is a dishwasher.

_____ Many modern kitchens have three major appliances in them.

2. _____ Another is a screwdriver.

_____ Several simple tools are useful to have around the house.

_____ The last is a wrench.

_____ A third is a pair of pliers.

_____ One is a hammer.

3. _____ The fourth was the video game and video tape system.

_____ What will be next?

_____ Let us look at five products that have developed from modern technology.

_____ The first development happened many years ago—the radio.

_____ We can find all five of them in our homes.

_____ The next development was the sound system, a combination of radio, stereo, and tape deck.

_____ The television was next, and it soon replaced the radio in popularity.

_____ The last and most recent development is the home computer.

J. LOGICAL WORD GROUPS

■ Directions: The following paragraph is from the article "SUPPLIES: A PERSONAL ESSAY." Read it quickly three times: first, in vertical logical word groups, next, in horizontal logical word groups, and finally in normal paragraph form.

a. Vertical

Some things
are necessary
in life.
I'm not talking
about the big things,
like food, water, shelter, and love.
I'm talking
about the little things,
the small necessities
that we have
in our homes, schools, and offices.
I'm talking
about the items
that we use
every day
without thinking.

b. Horizontal

Some things   are necessary   in life.   I'm not talking   about the big things, like food, water, shelter, and love.   I'm talking   about the little things,   the small necessities   that we have   in our homes, schools, and offices.   I'm talking about the items   that we use   every day   without thinking.

c. Normal Spacing

Some things are necessary in life. I'm not talking about the big things, like food, water, shelter, and love. I'm talking about the little things, the small necessities that we have in our homes, schools, and offices. I'm talking about the items that we use every day without thinking.

K. AGREE/DISAGREE

■ **Directions:**   Read the statements. Circle A if you agree with them. Circle D if you disagree with them. Discuss your answers in class.

		Agree	Disagree
1.	A quiet room is the best place to study.	A	D
2.	Physics and engineering students do not need a calculator.	A	D
3.	Pencils are better than pens for writing homework exercises.	A	D
4.	It is easy to listen to music and write homework exercises at the same time.	A	D
5.	Paper clips, scotch tape, and a stapler are necessary supplies for students.	A	D
6.	All people have certain supplies that they use every day or regularly.	A	D

L. GUESS

■ **Directions:**   Read the sentences. One word is underlined. Then read the three possible choices for the general meaning of the underlined word. Choose one and write the letter in the blank. Which parts of the sentences helped you guess?

1. I looked on all the shelves where I keep paper. I found typing paper, notebook paper, and drawing paper. But I didn't find one piece of <u>stationery</u>.

Stationery is _____.
a. a piece of furniture   b. a kind of paper   c. a kind of shelf

2. The staple remover is in the drawer with the staples, the scotch tape, and the paper clips.

A staple remover is _____.
a. an office supply   b. a garden supply   c. a game

3. The office does not have an electric typewriter, but it has a manual one.

The word *manual* describes _____.
a. a kind of office   b. a person   c. a kind of typewriter

4. Jay can fix anything in the house. He needs only a hammer, some nails, and a wrench.

A wrench is _____.
a. a kitchen utensil   b. a tool   c. a container

5. Optometrists use a lot of expensive, highly specialized equipment.

Optometrists are _____.
a. equipment   b. people   c. offices

6. I tried to tie the bicycle to the car with string, but the string was too thin and broke. Fortunately, I found a long piece of rope in the garage.

Rope is _____.
a. thick, heavy string   b. a tool   c. part of a bicycle

⊛
M. MAKING INFERENCES (Part 1)

Teacher: See note on making inferences in Part 2 of this exercise. For Part 1, write other lists that fit your students' interests and that use other vocabulary that you have covered. Let students use dictionaries and help each other with vocabulary. You may need to help them with vocabulary for the answers.

■ **Directions:** Read the lists of supplies, tools, and equipment. Each list represents a different kind of person. Try to identify the kind of person from the list. You may find more than one good answer. Discuss your answers in class.

EXAMPLE: paper
pencils
pens
notebook
textbooks
Who is it? *a student*

1. hammers
   nails
   screwdrivers
   saws
   drills

   Who is it? _____

2. chalk
   erasers
   textbooks
   grade book
   red pens and pencils
   dictionary
   folders

   Who is it? _____

3. combs
   brushes
   scissors
   shampoo
   towels
   hair dryers

   Who is it? _____

4. hoes
   rakes
   shovels
   hoses
   gloves

   Who is it? _____

⊛

N. MAKING INFERENCES (Part 2)

Teacher: Making inferences is difficult for students because it involves taking risks—making guesses about something that is not stated directly. The INFERENCE exercises are designed to help students develop confidence to take these risks and to make good guesses. **Note:** Most new verbs in this exercise can be demonstrated.

EXPLANATION: Sentences tell us some things *directly:*

I am hungry.

Sentences can tell us the same thing *indirectly:*

I did not eat breakfast or lunch today.   (*stated* information)

Question: How do I probably feel?
Answer: Hungry. (*unstated* information)

In this example, the answer *Hungry* is an **inference** (a guess) we can make from the stated information.

■ Directions: Now read the groups of sentences (stated information). Then read sentences a, b, and c. One of these sentences is a logical inference that we can make from the stated information. Choose the sentence that is the most logical inference and write the letter in the blank.

EXAMPLE: At 10:00 P.M., Richard picked up his books, papers, and pencils. He went to his room and closed the door. At midnight, he came out of his room and said, "Now I'm ready for the test tomorrow."

We can infer that ___*b*___.
a. Richard was sleeping.
b. Richard was studying.
c. Richard was watching TV.

1. Jay picked up the old scissors and went outside to the garden. I filled a vase with water.

We can infer that _____.
a. Jay went outside to work in the garden.
b. Jay and I are angry at each other.
c. Jay went outside to cut flowers for me.

2. Bobby got his comb. His mother got a sharp pair of scissors and a towel. They went outside to the backyard.

We can infer that _____.
a. Bobby and his mother are going to play a game.
b. Bobby's mother is going to cut his hair.
c. Bobby's mother is very angry at him and is going to punish him.

3. Last week five students were absent from class. They are back in class this week, but they are still coughing. Yesterday the teacher and three other students were absent.

We can infer that _____.
a. The teacher and the eight students are probably sick.
b. There is a school vacation.
c. The students do not like their class.

4. John broke his pencil in half. He tore up all the papers on his desk and threw them into the wastebasket. He turned off his calculator, closed his physics book, and left the room.

We can infer that _____.
a. John is a small child.
b. John is angry because he is having trouble with a physics problem.
c. John lives in a dormitory.

5. Pieces of broken glass were on the kitchen table and floor. Milk was everywhere. The little boy looked up at his mother and began to cry.

We can infer that _____.
a. The little boy spilled his milk and broke the milk glass.
b. The little boy broke a toy.
c. The mother has a lot of children.

⊛

O. CONNECTORS: Addition and Contrast

EXPLANATION: It is possible to connect the ideas in two sentences with a connecting word. Two kinds of connectors are connectors of **addition** and of **contrast.**

Teacher: This exercise teaches connectors for recognition rather than for production, and therefore does not focus on punctuation or on subtle syntactic and semantic differences within sets of connectors.

A. Addition. We can connect two ideas with a connector that shows addition: **and, also, furthermore,** and **in addition** are some examples. Look at these two ideas:

Idea 1: A computer is a useful machine for students.
Idea 2: A computer is a useful machine for teachers.

We can connect these two ideas in several ways:

1. A computer is a useful machine for students **and** teachers.
2. A computer is a useful machine for students. It is **also** useful for teachers.
3. A computer is a useful machine for students. **Furthermore** (or **In addition**), it is useful for teachers.

B. Contrast. Suppose we want to show that two ideas are in contrast (in opposition in some way). Then we can use a connector that shows contrast: **But** and **however** are two examples. Look at these two ideas:

Idea 1: Computers are expensive for most students. (a reason *not* to get one)
Idea 2: Computers are useful. (a reason *to* get one)

We can connect the two ideas like this:

1. Computers are expensive for most students, **but** they are useful machines.
2. Computers are expensive for most students; **however,** they are useful machines.

■ **Directions:**   Read the sentences. If they show addition, circle the abbreviation for addition (**add.**). If they show contrast, circle the abbreviation for contrast (**contr.**). Underline all the connectors of addition and contrast in the sentences.

		Addition	**Contrast**
EXAMPLE a:	Students use pencils every day. They <u>also</u> use pens.	(add.)	contr.
EXAMPLE b:	Grades are important to some students. <u>However,</u> other students don't care much about them.	add.	(contr.)

	Addition	**Contrast**
1. Jars are useful containers; however, they are breakable.	add.	contr.
2. Soft drinks come in bottles. They also come in recyclable cans.	add.	contr.
3. Most Americans have middle names, but they do not use them very often.	add.	contr.
4. Natural light is easy to study by. In addition, it creates a pleasant atmosphere in a room.	add.	contr.
5. Paper clips and staples are useful and practical items. Furthermore, they're not expensive.	add.	contr.
6. I used a typewriter for many years. Recently, however, I bought a small computer with a word processing program.	add.	contr.
7. Almost everybody has a camera, but very few people are good photographers.	add.	contr.
8. Aluminum is a lightweight metal. Furthermore, it can be recycled (i.e., used again).	add.	contr.

P. ACTIVITY: Making a Personal Supply List

■ **Directions:** What items are on your basic supply list at the present time? Make a list on paper of five or ten of the most important items to you. Discuss your finished lists in class. What differences do you find among your classmates?

Are there differences according to sex (male–female)?
Are there differences according to interests?
Are there differences according to age?
Are there differences according to profession?
Are there differences according to nationality?

EXTRA READING

Start Time _____

A MULTIPURPOSE ADJECTIVE

1   The word *sharp* can be used to describe many different things in your home,
2 classroom, and place of work. In this chapter, the writer talked about sharp pen-
3 cils, meaning pencils with a very fine point. The writer did not like dull pencils.

4   We can also use the word *sharp* to describe the blades of knives. Knives
5 also have points (ends). We can use the word *sharp* to describe a certain kind of
6 point, such as the sharp points of kitchen and steak knives. Scissors have blades,
7 too, and we can describe these blades as sharp or dull. Furthermore, the points
8 of scissors are either sharp or rounded, depending on the kind of scissors. Some
9 tools, such as saws, scrapers, and garden tools, also have blades. We can use the
10 words *sharp* and *dull* to describe the blades of these tools, too. Sharp knives,
11 scissors, and tools are easy to use. They cut things easily and quickly, without
12 effort.

13   The word *sharp* can also be used to describe the edges of furniture and of
14 some containers. For example, the edge of a table or desk can be sharp. In ad-
15 dition, we can describe the edge of an open can as sharp. The top of a can is
16 sometimes sharp enough to cut your hand. A piece of glass from a broken jar or
17 bottle is ordinarily very sharp.

18   Finally, we sometimes use the word *sharp* to describe people. A person who
19 *looks* (appears) sharp is very well dressed. A person who *is* sharp, on the other
20 hand, is intelligent, smart, and quick to learn and understand.

21   To summarize, the word *sharp* can be used to describe many kinds of objects
22 that have blades, points, and edges. When we use the word *sharp* to describe
23 people, it can mean nice-looking, well-dressed, or intelligent. It is an expressive
24 word because it can be used in many different ways.

TOTAL WORDS: 315   **End Time** _____

Reflection

Think or talk about these questions:

What word do you use in your language for *sharp,* as in a *sharp* knife? Can you use this word in other ways? Compare this word in your language with the description in the reading. Can you think of other words in your language or in English that can be used in several ways?

EXTRA READING 2

BIG SALE!!!
THIS WEEK ONLY

	WERE	THIS WEEK	WILL BE
pencils	10¢	5¢	15¢
ballpoint pens	79¢	50¢	$1.19
felt markers	89¢	60¢	$1.25
notebooks (lined)	$1.29	99¢	$1.59
typing paper (100 sheets)	$2.59	$2.00	$2.99
file folders	$1.19/doz.	$ .75/doz.	$1.69/doz.

ALL TEXTBOOKS   30% off

Coastview Institute Clothing

T-shirts	$4.99	$3.50	$6.00
sweatshirts	$6.99	$5.00	$8.50
running shorts	$6.50	$5.00	$7.75
jackets	$22.50	$18.00	$25.99

Answer the questions:

1. Where do you think you might find this advertisement?
2. Why are there three prices for every item?
3. How much did 200 sheets of typing paper cost last week?
4. How much are three felt markers this week?
5. If a textbook cost $15.00 last week, how much can buy it for today?
6. Do you have any clothing from your school? If so, what do you have?

Chapter 6
Substances

Jamal El-Ayoubi

PREREADING

Ⓟ **Activity:** Identifying Substances

Materials: If possible, examples of common substances and materials: a rock, a piece of wood, a piece of plastic, a piece of concrete, some sand and clay, a piece of some kind of metal. Other items from the classroom and from students' belongings: chairs, pencils and pens, notebook paper, wallets and purses, combs, rings, watches, shoes and socks, other clothing, coffee cups (paper, plastic, ceramic), cigarettes, lighters, etc.; paper and pencil for notes; bilingual dictionaries.

Teacher: You may want to use this exercise as a timed game. Encourage students to use their dictionaries *only* when no one in the group can provide a needed word. Some answers may not be known or clear-cut; let this fact stimulate discussion.

■ Directions: Form small groups. Put five or ten items in front of you. Follow these steps:

1. Appoint someone in your group to take notes.

2. What are the original substances (i.e., substances from nature in an original or basic form) of the items in your group? Discuss the possible answers. Use dictionaries *only* if no one in your group knows the word(s). Take notes.

EXAMPLE: **Items**   **Original Substances**
          pencil   wood, trees
                           graphite (a kind of clay)

Teacher: Step 3 is optional, but vocabulary of categories is important. See reading article.

---

3. Now try to categorize the items according to their materials (present form or original). Possible categories: natural/synthetic; animal/mineral/vegetable.

EXAMPLE: **Natural**   **Synthetic**
          pencil (wood)   comb (plastic)

4. Compare answers when all groups are finished.

Survey

■ Directions: Look at the article. Follow these directions from your teacher. Write your answers on paper or answer orally.

1. What is the title of the article?
2. What are the headings in this article?
3. How many substances are named in the headings?
4. Look at all the figures and diagrams. Notice that they show *changes* of substances into other substances.
5. What do the photographs show?

Scan

■ Directions: Look at the article. Follow these directions from your teacher. Write your answers on paper or answer orally. *Work quickly.*

1. Look at paragraph 2, **Background: Ways to Classify Substances.** Three ways to classify substances are mentioned. What are they?

2. Look at paragraph 3. What are the five groups of substances that this article is going to look at?

3. Look at the section on **Mineral Substances.** Find two examples of mineral substances.

4. Look at the section **Vegetable.** What vegetable substance is the topic of this section?

5. Look at the section **Petroleum.** What is another word for *petroleum?* (**Note:** This word is one of the words in parentheses.)

6. Look at the section **Synthetic Materials.** What is one example of a synthetic fiber?

7. Look at the conclusion. Find the word *man.* Is the word *man* written with a capital M or a small m?

Listen

■ **Directions:** Listen while your teacher reads all or part of the article out loud. Follow silently in your book.

Underline

Teacher: This exercise prepares students for the **Underline** exercises in *Strategies 2.* Continue using Key Words if you wish.

■ **Directions:** Open your book to the beginning of the article "SUBSTANCES." Your teacher will guide you through the underlining exercise. Follow these directions:

1. Paragraph 2 discusses three ways to classify substances. Circle the numbers.

2. Paragraph 3 tells you the five groups that this article will look at. Underline the names of the five groups.

3. The topic of paragraph 4 is a kind of natural substance. What is it? Underline one example of this substance.

4. What is the topic of paragraph 5? Underline two words.

5. What is the topic of paragraph 6? Underline one word.

6. Paragraph 7 is about metal ores. Underline the phrase *metal ores.* Now underline one or two examples of metals.

7. In paragraph 8, the word *vegetable* does not refer to food. What substance does it refer to?

8. Paragraph 9 talks about an important product that is made from wood. Underline the name of this product.

9. Paragraph 10 mentions several substances that come from animals. Underline one or two examples.

10. Paragraph 11 describes petroleum as a "naturally changed substance." Underline this phrase.

11. Paragraph 12 describes the process by which petroleum was made. Write the word *process* in the margin next to this paragraph.

12. The paragraph on synthetic materials describes how synthetic materials are made. Underline the phrase *taking apart the chemicals.* Underline the phrase *putting them back together.*

13. In the same paragraph, underline one example of a synthetic product.

14. Look at the conclusion. How many times is the word *change* (or a form of it) used?

Key Words

1 everything . . . made of some kind of substance
2 classify substances
      (1) origin . . . animal, vegetable, mineral
      (2) second
            natural or . . . man-made
      (3) third
            organic . . . inorganic
3 this article
    five groups
        mineral, vegetable, animal, petroleum, synthetics
4 mineral
    not . . . plants or animals
        clay
        pottery . . . bricks
5 glass . . . originates as sand
    solid to liquid
6 rock
  combinations of minerals
    concrete
7 metal ores
    iron, aluminum
8 plants
    wood
        for building and for burning
9   paper
10 animals
    fur or hair
    wool . . . from sheep
    leather
11 certain substances . . . cannot be classified in a simple way
  naturally changed substance . . . petroleum

12 millions of years ago . . . no petroleum
   plants and animals died
       thick layers
       pressure and heat
       petroleum
   nature changed one substance . . . into another
13 people also change substances
       petroleum
          refine
            oil, gasoline, and kerosene
14 some substances . . . do not . . . occur in nature
   synthetic materials
       taking apart the chemicals
       putting them back together . . . new way
          plastics
          fibers
15 nature changes many things
   Man changes many things

Skim

■ **Directions:** Look at the headings and diagrams. Review the **Survey** section. Quickly read the first section of the article, **Background: Ways to Classify Substances.** Read the first sentence of paragraph 3 (read to the period, not just to the colon). Look at your underlined words and phrases. Look at the list of key words.

Predict

■ **Directions:** Read the statements about the article. Put a T next to the ones that you believe are true, according to the article. Put an F next to the ones that you believe are false (not true about this article).

1. This article will probably discuss several common substances, such as rocks, plants, and petroleum.   _____

2. The most important topic in this article will be about synthetic materials.   _____

3. An important idea in this article will be that substances change from one form to another.   _____

4. The article will probably give examples of substances in the five categories of mineral, vegetable, animal, petroleum, and synthetics.   _____

5. The article will have a large section that describes how trees are changed into paper at a paper mill (factory).

SILENT READING

■ Directions: Now read the entire article carefully. Be prepared to discuss these questions:

1. What are more examples of substances around you?

2. Do all substances fit into the five categories that are discussed in the article?

3. What other things around you are made of substances in the five categories?

SUBSTANCES

1   Everything around us is made of some kind of substance. If you are sitting in a classroom, for example, you see many things. You see chairs, tables, and desks; books, paper, and pencils; windows, walls, ceilings, and floors. All of these things are made of different substances. What kinds of substances are there?

Background: Ways to Classify Substances

2   We can classify substances in several ways. Here are three: (1) Usually people classify substances into basic groups according to the origin of the substance: animal, vegetable, or mineral. (2) We can make a second distinction when we talk about substances: Are they natural or are they man-made? Natural substances originate[1] in nature and possibly are changed by nature. They are used in their natural form. Man-made substances are changed in some important way by people. Of course, sometimes it is difficult to separate natural and man-made substances. When a substance is completely man-made, it is called a synthetic substance. But even synthetic substances come originally from natural sources. (3) Finally, we can classify substances a third way according to two basic chemical groups: organic substances (from carbon compounds) and inorganic substances (all noncarbon compounds and elements).

3   In this article, we will look briefly at some substances from five groups: mineral, vegetable, animal, petroleum, and synthetics. These categories overlap.[2] We are not using them to classify all substances. The categories represent, simply, a useful way of looking at a few familiar substances.

---

[1]to originate (v) = to begin, have (their) origin in

[2]to overlap (v) = to have some parts in common; to be not completely separate

This pit mine is a source of minerals such as copper. (Courtesy of the Arizona Historical Society.)

Mineral Substances

4   A mineral is a natural substance. It is usually defined as an inorganic substance—one that does not originate from plants or animals. Gold, silver, rocks of various kinds—these are all minerals. A common mineral substance is clay. People can make clay into pots, vases, or bricks by changing the shape of the substance. Then, when the clay objects are heated to high temperatures, the chemical composition of the clay changes: The clay becomes hard and brittle. The result is pottery or very hard bricks. Pottery and bricks are made of clay, but they are not the same as clay. People have changed a natural substance into a man-made substance.

5   A similar process occurs in the making of glass. Glass originates as sand. Sand is another common mineral substance. Sometimes we can use sand in its natural state, such as when we mix it with other substances to make concrete. But when we heat pure sand to a high temperature, it changes form—from solid to liquid. When the liquid cools[3] and solidifies, the result is glass. Glass, then, is also a man-made substance that originates as a natural material.

---

[3]to cool (v) = to become colder

In this old photo of a smelter from the early 1900s, copper is being purified. (Courtesy of the Arizona Historical Society.)

6   Rock[4] is another common mineral substance in nature. Rocks are made of different combinations of minerals. Rocks are often used to build houses, bridges, and roads. Rocks are not always used alone, however. Small pieces of rock can be mixed with sand, water, and cement. This mixture becomes very hard when it solidifies; the end product is concrete. Concrete, a man-made substance, is a basic and common building material.

ROCK + SAND + CEMENT + WATER = CONCRETE

7   Certain kinds of rocks contain metal ores. These rocks are heated to extremely high temperatures in special factories (smelters). The metal part of the ore liquefies (melts), and the rock parts, which are all the nonmetal parts, are left behind. The liquid metal cools and solidifies, and the end product is a pure metal. Iron, aluminum, copper, silver, and gold are just a few examples of some

---

[4]rock (n, C and U): rock (U) = a descriptive name for a substance; rock (C) = a piece of the substance

useful and important metals that come from rocks. The products from them—steel girders, pots and pans, jewelry—are man-made, but the metals originate in nature.

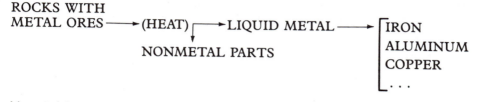

ROCKS WITH
METAL ORES ⟶ (HEAT) ┌⟶ LIQUID METAL ⟶ ⌈IRON
                            │   │ALUMINUM
                       ↓   │COPPER
          NONMETAL PARTS   ⌊ . . .

Vegetable

8   Many kinds of substances come from plants. We will discuss one common vegetable substance—wood. People cut down trees and use the wood to build houses and furniture (man-made products) and to burn for heat. For building purposes, the wood is cut up into carefully measured pieces (lumber). For burning, the wood is left in randomly sized pieces (logs). Wood for building and for burning is used in its natural state.

9   Wood has another important use: It is the main ingredient of paper. In fact, the paper in this book that you are reading right now was once a tree! The process of papermaking is too long and complicated to discuss in this short article.[5] We can say simply that trees enter a factory as logs—a substance from nature—and leave the factory as paper—a man-made substance.

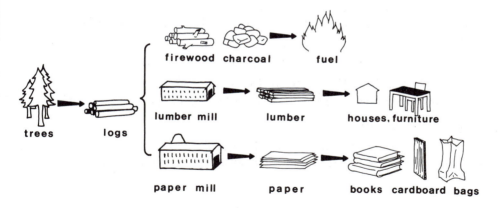

Animal

10   Animals are an important source of many common substances and materials. For example, we use the fur or hair of many animals to make clothing.

---

[5]See the Extra Reading on papermaking in this chapter.

Wool comes from sheep. Wool can be used in its natural state. However, we usually change the form of wool by spinning it into yarn.[6] Wool yarn is then made into clothing and blankets. Another example is leather. Leather is animal skin. Leather can be used either in its natural form (as rawhide) or it can be tanned.[7] Tanned leather is made into shoes, coats, hats, wallets and handbags, and so on.

Petroleum

11   There are certain substances that cannot be classified in a simple way as animal, vegetable, or mineral. Many substances are mixtures of these three groups. Furthermore, sometimes natural processes of the earth change one kind of substance (animal or vegetable) into another kind of substance (mineral). An example of such a naturally changed substance is petroleum (oil). Petroleum is essential[8] to humans in the world today. We use billions of gallons of this "black gold" every year.

12   Millions of years ago, however, there was no petroleum, but there were many plants and animals. Over thousands of years, the plants and animals died and formed thick layers. These layers were slowly covered over by land and by sea. Gradually, the tremendous pressure and heat of the earth changed these layers into petroleum. This process took millions of years. Thus, nature changed one substance (plants and animals) into another substance (petroleum).

13   But, as we have seen, people also change substances. In the case of petroleum, the help of people is necessary. Before we use petroleum, we need to break it down and refine it into its many usable products. Oil, gasoline, and kerosene are just a few examples of petroleum products that are the result of the refining process.[9]

PLANTS AND ANIMALS ⟶ LAYERS ⟶
PRESSURE, HEAT, AND TIME ⟶ PETROLEUM ⟶
REFINING PROCESS ⟶ OIL, GASOLINE, KEROSENE, ETC.

Synthetic Materials

14   People make many substances and materials: glass, concrete, metals, paper, and gasoline. These substances are from natural sources such as sand, rocks, and

---

[6]yarn (n, U) = thick thread made by twisting fibers of cotton, wool, or synthetic materials together. Thread and yarn are similar to string; they are used in sewing.

[7]Animal skin is changed into leather by a process called *tanning*. In this process, animal skin is soaked in a liquid that contains tannin. Tannin comes from the bark of trees.

[8]essential (adj) = extremely important; necessary

[9]Petroleum is changed into usable products in a factory called a *refinery.* To refine a product is to separate the pure substances from the impure ones.

plants. Some substances, however, do not ever occur in nature and are made only by people. Such substances are called *synthetic materials.* Synthetic materials are made by taking apart the chemicals in natural substances, changing the chemicals, and putting them back together in a totally new way.[10] This process takes place in the chemistry laboratory. Many synthetic products—plastics and synthetic fibers such as nylon and polyester—are made from petroleum. In fact, the list of products made with synthetic materials is endless: furniture, clothing, utensils, containers, toys, appliances, paints. Today's modern world is a synthetic world.

Conclusion: Man the Changer

15   Nature changes many things: seeds into plants, plants and animals into petroleum, mountains into rocks, rocks into sand. But Man[11] changes many things, too. He uses the forces of nature, such as heat and pressure, in a controlled way to help change one substance into another. He uses chemistry to make new substances. He starts with the substances in nature, changes them, and makes houses, containers, utensils, books, cities, roads, and art. No other animal on earth changes so many things!

EXERCISES _____

A. COMPREHENSION CHECK: True or False

■ Directions: Read the statements about the article. Write T after the statements that are true according to the article. Write F after statements that are false.

1. This article categorizes substances in a useful way but not in a scientific way.   _____

2. The article describes, in a very simple way, how we get petroleum.   _____

3. There is a big section in the article on papermaking.   _____

_____

[10]*To synthesize* means to put different parts together.

[11]Man (n, U) = humankind; people. *Man* in this context does not mean *male,* but people in general. We use the pronouns *he* and *him;* the plural form does not exist. The context of the sentence will tell you whether *Man* = people or *man* = male. This use of the word *man* is still common. However, many writers are trying to substitute other words for *Man,* such as *people, humans,* and *humankind.*

4. The article tries to classify all substances.   _____

5. Synthetic materials are made through chemistry.   _____

6. The article classifies clay, sand, and rocks as organic substances.   _____

7. A main idea of the article is that many substances are the result of natural or man-made changes.   _____

B. COMPREHENSION CHECK: Discuss

■ **Directions:**   As a class or in small groups, discuss the following questions:

1. What kinds of substances from nature can we change into useful products?

2. In your opinion, what is the simplest substance that is discussed in the article? What is the most complex substance? Can you explain your opinion?

3. Discuss the questions from the SILENT READING section.

C. COMPREHENSION CHECK: Recall

■ **Directions:**   How much of the article can you remember? With your whole class or with one or two classmates, recall as much as you can. Try to recall in **categories;** it is easier to remember more this way.

D. SELECTIVE READING: Categorize, Underline

■ **Directions:**   Read the line of words. One of the words is the name of a category or group to which all the other words belong. Underline the word that is the category for the other words. Work quickly.

1. wood   natural substances   petroleum   gold   sand

2. nylon   polyester   plastics   synthetics   dacron

3. paper products   cardboard   notebook paper   paper bags

4. knife blades   aluminum cans   metal products   razor blades

5. rocks   sand   minerals   clay   ores

6. metals   iron   gold   copper   aluminum   silver

7. to heat   to cool   to change   to solidify   to liquefy   to melt

8. paper mill   oil refinery   smelter   factory   tannery

(*)

E. SELECTIVE READING: Identify Antonyms

■ **Directions:** Look at the word in parentheses. Then read the sentence. In the sentence, there is an **antonym** of the word in parentheses. An antonym is a word that has an **opposite** (or nearly opposite) meaning to another word. Underline the antonym in the sentence. Work quickly.

> EXAMPLE: (large) Diamonds are beautiful, relatively <u>small</u> stones that have an organic origin.

1. (man-made) Many substances are natural, but others are synthetic.
2. (dull) Most cooks prefer to use sharp knives.
3. (solidify) It is necessary to liquefy very pure sand in order to make glass.
4. (stiff) Clay is a stiff, malleable substance, unlike petroleum, which is liquid.
5. (quiet) Factories such as paper mills and oil refineries are large, noisy, and smelly.
6. (cool, v) If we heat metal ores to a high temperature, the metal liquefies.

(*)

F. SELECTIVE READING: Identify Main Clauses

Teacher: There is so much extra information that can be attached to main clauses and so much terminology to go with it that students at this level can be overwhelmed. Recommendation: Teach gradually and by examples; introduce and use terminology at your discretion.

EXPLANATION: Look at the following sentence:

> Wood, which is an important building material in many parts of the world, comes from trees.

This sentence is long. It has two parts:

> 1. main idea—Wood . . . comes from trees.
> 2. extra information— . . . , which is an important building material in many parts of the world, . . .

Now look at this sentence:

> A main clause (sometimes called an independent clause) can exist as a complete sentence.

This sentence also has two parts:

> 1. main idea—A main clause . . . can exist as a complete sentence.
> 2. extra information— . . . (sometimes called an independent clause) . . .

Extra information can be marked in several ways. In the first example, the word *which* and the commas mark the extra information. In the second example, the parentheses mark the extra information. Dashes (—) and colons (:) can also mark extra information. In all cases, the grammar of the sentence can tell us which part of the sentence is the main idea and which part is extra information.

One of the most important tasks in reading is to identify and follow main clauses, and not to confuse the main ideas with the extra information. Let's practice.

■ **Directions:** Read the sentences quickly. Identify and underline the main clause in each sentence. Do not worry if you do not understand every word.

EXAMPLE: This chapter (like the other chapters in this unit) is about things.

1. Textbooks—unlike novels—have indexes and tables of contents.

2. Chalk, a soft limestone substance found in nature, is a basic supply in most classrooms.

3. The "lead" in pencils is actually graphite (a soft form of carbon occurring in nature as a kind of clay).

4. Good furniture—the kind that is made from the best materials—is expensive.

5. This article looks at substances from five groups: mineral, vegetable, animal, petroleum, and synthetics.

6. We can classify substances as organic (substances from carbon compounds) or inorganic (all noncarbon compounds and elements).

7. Many synthetic products—various kinds of plastics and synthetic fibers such as nylon and polyester—are made from petroleum.

G. VOCABULARY STUDY

Teacher: Encourage students to use English-English dictionaries. Review alphabetizing if necessary. Help students learn what information their dictionaries provide (each one is a little different) and how they display it. In particular, remind students that they will usually be looking for *one* part of speech and *one* definition.

■ **Directions:** Find three to five words in the reading article that you would like to learn about. Your words may be different from those of your classmates. Ask yourself these questions about each word:

Before you use your dictionary:

1. What kind of word is it? Noun? Verb? Adjective? Other? (You will know this by how the word is used in its sentence.)

2. Does the word refer to or describe an object? A person? An idea? A place? An action? Something else?

3. Can you get an idea about what the word means from the sentence it is in? From the paragraph?

4. Do any of your classmates know what this word means? Ask them.

5. Can your teacher help you understand this word?

When you use your dictionary:

1. Find the word.

2. Check the **part of speech** (noun, verb, adjective . . .) to see that it is the same as your word.

3. If your word has more than one definition in the dictionary, find the one that seems to match the meaning of your word in the reading article.

4. If you have a vocabulary notebook, write down the word, the part of speech, the sentence from the reading article, and one meaning.

H. SCAN: Underline or Take Notes

Teacher: Students should not attempt to comprehend every word in this exercise. Advise them to choose one adjective if a sentence has two or more that describe the same substance.

■ **Directions (choose A or B):**

A. Read the sentences quickly. Each sentence names and describes a substance. Underline the name of the substance and *one* adjective that describes the substance.

B. Read the sentences quickly. Each sentence names and describes a substance. Write the name of the substance and one adjective that describes the substance on a piece of paper or in the margin of your book.

> EXAMPLES: (A) <u>Chalk</u> is a <u>soft</u> substance that is found in nature.
>
> (B) Chalk—soft

1. Cardboard is a thick paper product that is used to make boxes.

2. Because glass is breakable, it is not often used for shampoo bottles.

3. Concrete has a very rough texture.

4. Trees provide us with wood, which is one of nature's most useful substances.

5. Containers that are made of plastic are both lightweight and unbreakable.

6. Steel (iron treated with heat and carbon) is an extremely strong and durable material.

7. In its natural form, petroleum is a thick, black liquid.

8. Many blackboard erasers are made of felt, which is a soft material made from wool and fur or hair.

(✱)

I. WORD FORMS: Prefixes and Suffixes

EXPLANATION: Look at the following two adjectives:

common   *un*common

They are the same except for the prefix *un-*. *Un-* means *not*. It has a negative meaning. Therefore, *uncommon* means *not common*. The prefix *in-* can also mean *not*.

Teacher: Do not attempt to explain all affixes at this point! Students will learn them gradually. **Note:** An affix is added to an existing word. The *in-* of *interesting* is not an affix.

Look at the chart of adjectives:

Affirmative Meaning	Prefix	Negative Meaning
breakable common complicated important interesting	*un-*	unbreakable uncommon uncomplicated unimportant uninteresting
expensive flexible formal organic	*in-*	inexpensive inflexible informal inorganic

We can also add a suffix to the end of a word and change the word's meaning. The following adjectives have a suffix attached to the noun *use:*

use*ful*   use*less*

The suffix *-ful* means *with,* or *full of*. It has an affirmative meaning. The suffix *-less* means *without*. It has a negative meaning. Look at the chart of adjectives:

Noun Forms	Affirmative Meaning	Negative Meaning
	-ful	*-less*
care	careful	careless
cheer	cheerful	cheerless
color	colorful	colorless
use	useful	useless
count	——	countless
end	——	endless

■ **Directions:** Read the sentences. Fill in the blanks with the logically correct form of the adjectives in parentheses. If you have trouble, look at the meaning of the sentence again.

EXAMPLE: I did not talk in class today because the conversation was *un-interesting* for me. (interesting/uninteresting)

1. The walls of the supermarket were covered with large pictures of food in bright reds, greens, blues, and yellows. The pictures gave the supermarket a _____ _____ atmosphere. (colorful/colorless)

2. Most people cannot buy gold because it is too _____. (expensive/inexpensive)

3. Most students believe that homework is an _____ part of their studies. (important/unimportant)

4. Plastic is a _____ material for containers because it is _____. (useful/useless) (breakable/unbreakable)

5. Sand is a very _____ mineral substance. (common/uncommon)

6. _____ substances contain carbon. (Organic/Inorganic)

7. Occasionally the atmosphere in the classroom is _____ because students feel sad and homesick. (cheerful/cheerless)

8. Most people believe that the American life-style is _____. (formal/informal)

J. CONNECTORS: Addition and Contrast (Review)

■ **Directions:** Review the exercise on connectors in Chapter 5 if necessary. Then read the sentences. Connect the two parts of the sentences (or the two sentences) with an appropriate connector. Choose from the list. Work in groups or alone. **Note:** Watch for clues such as punctuation and location of the blank to help you make a good choice. (See Chapter 5 for some models.)

EXAMPLE: Sand is used to make concrete. It is *also* used to make glass.

Addition	**Contrast**
and	but
also	however
furthermore	
in addition	

1. Gold is a beautiful metal. _____, it is difficult to find it in large quantities.

2. Nature changes many substances. Man _____ changes substances.

3. Synthetic materials are useful in many ways, _____ they can be dangerous if they burn.

4. Ceramic pottery is beautiful; _____, it is brittle and breakable.

5. Aluminum cans are lightweight. _____, they can be recycled.

6. Most clear glass is relatively inexpensive. Good quality colored glass, _____ _____, is very expensive.

7. We can use wood for building and burning purposes. _____, we can use it to make paper.

K. ORDER: Process

■ **(A) Directions:**   Look at the lists of words. The words describe different stages (moments) or materials in a process or series of events. They are in random order. Put a number by each word to show where it belongs in the process.

EXAMPLE: _2_ shaping of clay
_3_ heat
_1_ clay
_4_ pottery

1. _____ pressure, heat, time

_____ gasoline, kerosene

_____ petroleum

_____ refinery

_____ layers

_____ plants and animals

2. _____ cooling

_____ sand

_____ glass

_____ liquefying

_____ heating

_____ solidifying

3. _____ logs

_____ trees

_____ houses

_____ lumber mill

_____ lumber

_____ builders and carpenters

4. _____ yarn

_____ sheep

_____ wool

_____ clothing

_____ shearing (cutting wool from sheep)

Teacher: Students will need to watch for a sequence of vocabulary in part B. The first mention of a noun will usually not have the article *the,* but the second will. These exercises can be done as strip stories (see explanation in Information for Teachers) for maximum communication.

■ **(B) Directions:** Read the sentences. They describe the events in a process. They are in random order. Put a number by each sentence to show the correct order of the events.

1. WHERE WOOL COMES FROM

_____ Then the wool is washed very well.

_____ The yarn is finally ready to make into cloth.

_____ First sheep are sheared of all their wool.

_____ Next the clean wool is spun into yarn.

2. THE MAKING OF PETROLEUM

_____ The plants and animals formed layers that were gradually covered by land and by sea.

_____ Millions of years ago countless plants and animals died.

_____ The result was the product we know today as petroleum (oil).

_____ During these years, heat and pressure changed the plants and animals into a new substance.

_____ Millions of years passed.

3. PAPERMAKING

_____ The chips are then ground into very small fibers (pulp) by a chemical process.

_____ The clean, bleached pulp is made into large sheets.

_____ Papermaking begins with trees.

(*Continued on next page.*)

_____ The finished paper is ready to be cut and packaged.

_____ The trees are cut into small pieces called *chips*.

_____ The pulp is washed and bleached many times.

_____ The sheets are pressed and dried.

L. FACT OR OPINION

■ **Directions:** Read the statements. Circle F if you believe that the statement is a fact. Circle O if you believe that the statement is an opinion.

		Fact	Opinion
1.	Plastic is a petroleum product.	F	O
2.	Rocks, clay, sand, and metals are mineral substances.	F	O
3.	Nylon, dacron, and polyester clothing is more comfortable than clothing made of cotton or other natural fibers.	F	O
4.	Gold is more expensive than silver.	F	O
5.	Gold is more beautiful than silver.	F	O
6.	Glass containers are better than plastic containers.	F	O
7.	The processes of making paper, refining petroleum, and making steel are complicated.	F	O
8.	The processes of making paper, refining petroleum, and making steel are interesting.	F	O

M. ANALOGIES

■ **Directions:** Complete the analogies. Circle the best choice in the line, then write the word in the blank.

1. scissors:cut   _____:**sharpens**

    knife   pencil   pencil sharpener   supply

2. true:false   **black:**_____

    white   color   different   opposite

3. cat:animal   _____:**machine**

    technology   computer   engineer   scientific

4. container:bottle _____:**hammer**

nail tool metal build

5. synonym:same **antonym:**_____

similar true false different

6. plant:vegetable **rock:**_____

mineral organic natural concrete

7. petroleum:synthetics _____:**paper**

wood supply man-made process

8. paper:trees _____:**sand**

pottery glass oil rocks

N. ACTIVITY: Filling in a Preference Chart

■ **Directions:** **A.** What kinds of materials do you like? Look at the chart on the next page. It shows a list of materials (left) and a list of common household items (top). Check the boxes that show your preferences of materials for each item. You may check more than one box per item if an item is made of several materials. Add materials or items to the list if you wish. Compare your preferences in class. Can you explain your choices?

B. Some of the choices on the chart are *not possible.* For example, eating utensils (knives, forks, spoons, chopsticks) are probably never made of cloth. Put an X in all of the boxes that you believe are *impossible* choices. Do you and your classmates agree?

EXTRA READING

Start Time _____

THE PROCESS OF PAPERMAKING

1   Paper is not a substance that is found in nature. It is a substance that is
2 made by people. The process of papermaking was invented by the Chinese 2,000
3 years ago. The four main steps of the papermaking process are the same today
4 as they were then. First the materials for making the paper are prepared. Then
5 a layer of the wet material is formed on a special machine. Next, the water is
6 removed from the material. Finally, the layer of material is dried and finished.
7   Paper can be made from several different kinds of materials. The most com-
8 mon materials are vegetable fibers. Today, ninety percent of all paper is made

Materials Preference Chart

MATERIAL \ ITEM	FURNITURE			UTENSILS			CLOTHES	JEWELRY	
	sofa	chair	table	pots and pans	eating utensils	cups and plates		ring	
wood									
plastic									
leather									
ceramic (clay)									
aluminum									
stainless steel									
glass									
cloth (natural)									
cloth (synthetic)									
silver									
gold									

9 from wood. Sometimes other vegetable fibers are used: cotton and linen rags,
10 straw, and wastepaper. Occasionally paper is made from mineral and synthetic
11 material such as gypsum, asbestos, and synthetic polymers.
12   Let us look at the papermaking process more closely. The most complicated
13 part of the process is the preparation of the basic material called **pulp.** Pulp is
14 made from wood. Pulp consists of the individual fibers of cellulose from wood.
15 A tree is about fifty percent cellulose.
16   To change wood into pulp, logs from trees are first cut into small pieces
17 called **chips.** The chips are then ground into *very* small pieces. These very small
18 pieces are "cooked" and treated in different chemicals until the noncellulose
19 parts dissolve and are washed away. The cellulose fibers are then washed many
20 times, and usually bleached to make them white.
21   Next, the pulp fibers are mixed with water. This mixture flows over a screen.
22 The extra water goes through the screen, and the solid pulp stays on top of the
23 screen.
24   In the last steps of the papermaking process, this wet, solid layer of pulp
25 is carefully pressed and dried. Special machines do this with heat and pressure.
26 The final result is paper, which is ready to be cut and packaged.
27   A simplified flowchart of the papermaking process might look like this:

28   TREES - - - ► LOGS - - - ► CHIPPING - - - ►
29   "COOKING" TO MAKE PULP - - - ►
30 WASHING - - - ► BLEACHING - - - ► SCREENING - - - ► PRESSING - - - ►
31   DRYING - - - ► CUTTING - - - ► PACKAGING

TOTAL WORDS: 345   **End Time** _____

Reflection

Think or talk about these questions:

How many different kinds of paper do you use every day? Is paper an important part of your life? (Think carefully about how many things around you are made of paper.) Do you believe that there are enough trees in the world for all the paper that is made? What do you think will happen in the future if we don't have enough trees?

EXTRA READING 2

WHAT IS A TOXIC SUBSTANCE?

To the scientist, a chemical and a substance are the same thing. Water, salt, and sugar are chemicals. Petroleum and proteins are both chemicals. Food, rocks, and air are chemicals. Some chemicals are simple, like the element oxygen, which is made of just one kind of atom. Other chemicals, like proteins, are more complex because they are made of many kinds of atoms. Chemicals can be organic (containing carbon atoms) or inorganic (containing no carbon atoms). Chemicals can also be natural or synthetic.

Most chemicals—the food we eat, the substances in nature, medicines—are beneficial. In other words, they make our lives better and help us in different ways. Many of these chemicals are made in nature and are not dangerous to our health. But now many chemicals are made in the laboratory. They are man-made. Such synthetic chemicals are more dangerous than natural chemicals because they are foreign to the environment. Many synthetic chemicals are toxic: They

Martha Casanave

can make us sick or even kill us. Toxic chemicals can cause problems in the environment by killing plants, animals, and fish.

At the present time, industrial societies have a problem: where to store all the toxic chemicals produced by industries. When we dispose of them (i.e., throw them away), they do not just disappear into nature. Some industries store toxic chemicals in metal drums, but the problem remains: where to store the drums. Furthermore, old drums can leak. If the drums are stored underwater, toxic chemicals can leak into the water. If they are stored underground, toxic chemicals can leak into the ground and into groundwater supplies. Some people have suggested that we store toxic chemicals on the moon. Other people say that we must stop producing toxic chemicals.

We need to ask some serious questions about toxic substances. First, how beneficial is each toxic substance to industry and medicine? Second, how toxic is each substance? Third, how much of each toxic substance can be in the environment "safely"? Fourth, how can we store and dispose of toxic substances so that they do not leak into the environment later? And finally, do we *really* want to put toxic substances into space?

Answer the questions:

1. Check all the places where you might read this article.

_____ in a textbook	_____ in a children's story
_____ in a newspaper	_____ in a dictionary
_____ in a computer magazine	_____ in a science magazine
_____ in a college catalog	_____ in a novel
_____ in an environmental magazine	

2. Look up the word *poison* in your dictionary. Find a synonym (a word with a similar meaning) for the word poison in the article.

3. Check the statements that are *probably true* about the writer of the article:

_____ He or she might be a scientist.

_____ He or she might be an environmentalist.

_____ He or she might be an industrialist.

_____ He or she is worried about toxic substances in the environment.

_____ He or she believes that toxic substances are beneficial.

_____ He or she believes that toxic substances are dangerous.

————— He or she is not worried about where industry stores toxic substances.

————— He or she thinks that putting toxic chemicals on the moon is a bad idea.

4. The writer tells us in the second paragraph that natural substances and medicines are not dangerous to our health. But what can happen if
   a. you eat too much salt?
   b. you do not eat enough salt?
   c. you eat too much meat?
   d. you take too much aspirin?
   e. you eat too much sugar?

5. Do you agree with the writer's ideas about toxic substances?

APPENDIX 1

How to Calculate Reading Speed: Words per Minute (WPM)

1. Record Start Time (on the minute if possible).
2. Record End Time to the nearest second.
3. Subtract Start Time from End Time (result = Reading Time).
4. Change Reading Time to seconds by multiplying the number of minutes by 60. Add extra seconds.
5. Divide number of seconds into number of words (result = Words per Second).
6. Multiply Words per Second by 60 (result = WPM).

EXAMPLE: Total Words in Extra Reading = 400
Reading Time = 2 minutes 20 seconds

Change Reading Time to seconds:
2 (minutes) × 60 (seconds) = 120 seconds
120 seconds + 20 seconds = 140 seconds

Divide number of seconds into number of words:
$$\frac{400 \text{ (number of words)}}{140 \text{ (number of seconds)}} = 2.9 \text{ (Words per Second)}$$

Multiply Words per Second by 60:
2.9 × 60 = 171.4 WPM

APPENDIX 2

Key Content Words

These words are taken from the Key Words lists and reading article footnotes. **Note:** In this list, *-ing* words are nouns or adjectives and *-ed* words are adjectives, reflecting their use in the readings. Verbs are listed in their infinitive form.

Teacher: Parts of speech are not given in this list. Check with the main reading article in each chapter to see how the Key Words are used *in context* (chapter numbers follow each word).

Many words, of course, can be used as several parts of speech. Sometimes the stress changes (*décrease* [n] vs. *decréase* [v]), or the pronunciation is different ([n] *use* vs. [v] *use*). In other cases words are pronounced identically: exercise, bottle, group, name, work. Students probably learn such words best from context, rather than from a list. You will need to address these issues in the most appropriate way for your own class.

(word–chapter number)

age–3
alphabetical–2
aluminum–6
animal–6
another–6
arrangement–3
article–2, 4, 6
atmosphere–3
back–2
bag–4
basic–4, 5
blackboard–3
book–2, 3
bottle–4

bottleneck–4
box–4
brick–6
brush–4
budget–3
building–6
burning–6
can–4
cap–4
cardboard–4
carton–4
ceramic–4
chair–3
chalk–3

to change–6
chapter–2
chemical–6
circle–3
class–3
to classify–6
classroom–3
clay–6
closet–3
color–3
combination–6
common–1
concrete–6
container–4

contents–2
to cool–6
cultural–3
cupboard–3
cylindrical–4
desk–3
to die–6
difference–3
different–3, 4, 5
drawer–5
e.g.–4
eraser–3
essential–6
etc.–4
everything–6
exercise–2
factor–3
family–1
fibers–6
fifth–5
finally–3
first–1, 3, 5
flexible–4
foil–4
folding–4
footnote–2
form–1
fourth–5
front–2
fur–6
furniture–3
gasoline–6
glass–4, 6
good–5
group–6
hair–6
heading–2
heat–6
holder–5
home–4
hundred–5

i.e.–4
illustration–2
index–2
to influence–3
informal–1
information–2
inorganic–6
introduction–2
iron–6
jar–4
to keep–5
kerosene–6
label–1
large–3, 5
last–1
layer–6
leather–6
lectern–3
lid–4
life–4
lighting–3
to like–1
liquid–6
list–2, 5
location–3
made (to make)–6
main–3
Man–6
man-made–6
map–3
market–4
material–6
metal–4, 6
middle–1
million–6
mineral–6
money–3
mouth–4
name–1
natural–6
nature–6

necessary–5
neck–4
new–2
nickname–1
number–2
object–3
to occur–6
oil–6
one–6
to open–4
ore–6
organic–6
organization–2
origin–1, 6
to originate–6
to overlap–6
page–2
pair–5
paper–3, 4, 5, 6
paper clip–5
part–2
pen–3
pencil–3, 5
people–6
person–5
petroleum–6
picture–3
plant–6
plastic–4
pottery–6
practical–4
to practice–2
to prepare–2
prereading–2
pressure–6
profession–4
purpose–3, 5
to put (back)–6
quality–5
to read–2
reason–3

rectangular–3, 4
to refine–6
rock–6
round–3
row–3
same–3
sand–6
school–4
scissors–5
to seal–4
sealing–4
second–3, 5, 6
semicircle–3
seventh–5
sharp–5
sharpener–5
sheep–6
shelf–3
short–4
similar–3
similarity–3

simple–6
sixth–5
small–3
solid–6
some–6
speaker–1
square–3, 4
stapler–5
string–5
student–3
subheading–2
substance–6
summary–2, 4
supply–5
to synthesize–6
synthetic–6
table–3
to take (apart)–6
tape–5
teacher–3, 5
to tell–5

textbook–2
thick–6
thing–5
third–3, 5, 6
title–1, 2
topic–2
traffic jam–4
use–5
to use–5
vegetable–6
vocabulary–2
to want–5
wide–4
wood–4, 6
wool–6
work–4
to work–5
writer–5
yarn–6

INDEX